Knight

de la bataille enuis se comba
tent a ost assemble grant
sene est soprement contraî
dre plus par fam que par fer

Cy comence la seconde po
De ce chapitre qui traitte
cauteles qui autrement
guerre. Prologue

l cesti deuxieme p
tie apres ce que a
uons deuise selon
nestre principalement les
maineres que jadis tenopent

les vaillant conquereu
du monde es fais darm
en leure conqueistes pou
que ceulx se seurent bien
der et aidie de plus dune

MICHAEL PRESTWICH

Knight

The Medieval Warrior's (Unofficial) Manual

with 113 illustrations, 22 in color

Thames & Hudson

In memory of Lucy Thweng,
who knew many knights

Michael Prestwich is Professor Emeritus at the University of Durham.
His books include *War, Politics and Finance under Edward I*; *The Three
Edwards*; *Edward I*; *Armies and Warfare in the Middle Ages: the English
Experience*; and *Plantagenet England, 1225-1360*. He contributed to
The Medieval World at War, published by Thames & Hudson.

HALF-TITLE *One of the Knights Templar at the end of the 13th century.*

TITLE PAGE *Christine de Pizan, from the* Livre des Faits d'Armes
et de Chevalerie, *15th century.*

PAGES 4-5 *A typical late medieval longsword.*

First published in 2010 in hardcover in the United States
of America by Thames & Hudson Inc., 500 Fifth Avenue,
New York, New York 10110

thamesandhudsonusa.com

Library of Congress Catalog Card Number 2009936406

ISBN 978-0-500-25160-7

Printed and bound in China by Toppan Leefung

†able of Con†en†s

I ‡ *A Knight's World* 6

II ‡ *Upbringing & Training* 13

III ‡ *Becoming a Knight* 23

IV ‡ *Arms, Armour & Horses* 36

V ‡ *Orders of Knighthood* 54

VI ‡ *Recruitment & Retinues* 63

VII ‡ *Tournaments & Jousts* 79

VIII ‡ *Campaigning* 93

IX ‡ *Crusade* 108

X ‡ *Mercenaries* 117

XI ‡ *Ladies & Damsels* 126

XII ‡ *Siege* 136

XIII ‡ *Battle* 148

XIV ‡ *Ransoms & Booty* 174

XV ‡ *Piety & Memory* 186

Map of Medieval Europe 194 ‡ *Glossary* 196 ‡ *Timeline* 197
Further Reading 198 ‡ *Sources of Quotations* 200
Sources of Illustrations 203 ‡ *Index* 205

I

A Kṇiɢʜᴛ's Woʀʟᴅ

*Every man who does well in this military vocation
should be prized and honoured.*

GEOFFROI DE CHARNY, *THE BOOK OF CHIVALRY*, 1350–51

✠   ✠   ✠

magine yourself on a splendid charger, encased by gleaming armour, brandishing sword, lance and shield. Or picture yourself at court, renowned for your bravery and surrounded by beautiful damsels. Of course you want to be a knight. But this is not easy in the early 15th century. It is not just a simple matter of buying a horse and a suit of armour; there is much you must learn. Some books will teach you about the ideals of chivalry, but they do not provide the practical advice you need if you are determined to live – and quite possibly die – for glory on the battlefield. That is what this manual will give you.

Since the start of the 14th century we have been living in an age of war throughout Europe, and the mounted knight is the most magnificent figure on the battlefield. Much more than just a soldier; he should be the epitome of chivalry, a paragon of virtue. Prowess, loyalty, generosity and mercy are among his guiding principles.

Yet there is a difficult balance to be struck between the ideals and the practicalities of warfare. The knight is challenged and often defeated on the battlefield by common soldiers armed with bow and pike; he fights on foot more often than on horseback, and the guiding principles of chivalry often seem in reality to become those of guile, deceit, profit and cruelty.

The advice in this manual is derived from the practical experience of knights and men-at-arms. It is not based on romantic chivalric literature;

The knights of today take their inspiration from a heroic past. This image shows the knightly followers of the renowned hero Godfrey de Bouillon, one of the leaders of the 11th-century First Crusade, riding off to battle.

tales of King Arthur and other mythical heroes may help to keep you amused during a siege or a lull between battles, and may even mirror knightly behaviour on occasion, but they are hardly a realistic guide.

This is not a book of instruction for the sort of knight who may go on one or two campaigns, but who spends most of his time managing his estates, playing his part in local politics and attending law courts. This is a manual for the knight at war.

War

War is complex; it is not a simple matter of gaily adorned knights charging into battle. For a start, it involves a great deal of organization. States need to have systems of taxation to raise the money for armies up to 30,000 men strong. Sophisticated credit systems operated by international merchant banking houses are required to enable rulers and cities to meet the short-term needs of expensive campaigns. Armies need supply systems to provide the hundreds of tons of food and thousands of gallons of drink that they require. Siege warfare involves the deployment of up-to-date military hardware. Internationally recognized conventions, amounting to a law of war, regulate conflict and its aftermath. Within all this, there is a great deal of scope for ambitious individuals to develop knightly careers. The opportunities are there for you to grasp.

ABOVE *At Crécy in 1346 the English triumphed over the French.*

OPPOSITE *At Courtrai in 1302 Flemish townspeople also defeated a great French army.*

Where can you fight?

War is deeply ingrained in Europe, and as a knight, you will have no difficulty finding employment. Conflict is endemic between states, but is most deeply entrenched between France and England, with the war that began in 1337 and seems likely to last for 100 years. That is a tricky situation; from one point of view the kings of England are rebellious vassals of the French rulers, and from another, they are justified by descent in calling themselves kings of France. At times local rivalries and internal disputes make it seem more of a French civil war than a war between nations. Great battles have punctuated this war, above all the three great English victories of Crécy in 1346, Poitiers ten years later, and most recently Agincourt in 1415.

French ambitions in the Low Countries have also led to much fighting, from the battle of Courtrai in 1302 when Flemish urban forces defeated the French host, to that of Roosebeke in 1382, when the French were triumphant. Similarly, English designs upon Scotland have resulted in many campaigns. English successes under Edward I were overturned under his successor Edward II at Bannockburn in 1314; but during the following reign the king of Scots, David II, was captured at Neville's Cross in 1346.

Another struggle for independence has been that of the Swiss, whose infantry troops were more than a match for Habsburg forces at Morgarten in 1315, and Sempach in 1386.

In Italy, there is constant rivalry between cities, with Milan, Florence and Venice the most powerful in a world of shifting allegiances and frequent campaigning. The wealth of the cities, and the opportunities for fighting, are a magnet drawing in soldiers from Germany and elsewhere. Further south, the Papacy is not only a spiritual power, but also a player in the complex politics of the peninsula. The kingdom of Naples, whose dynasty hailed from Anjou in France, is in conflict with Sicily, ruled by the Aragonese king.

The Iberian peninsula has recently offered further potential for an ambitious knight, particularly with dynastic complications in Castile in the 1360s, and the Portuguese struggle for independence in the 1380s.

At the other end of Europe, the Baltic has seen German eastward expansion taking place for many years; the fiercest opponents of which are the Lithuanians. There are ample opportunities to join in the struggle against them, under the leadership of the Teutonic Knights. This is a religious crusade; there are other crusading opportunities available in the Mediterranean world, but success there is hard to come by.

Individual careers

The potential for a military knight is best demonstrated by outlining the careers of three of the key individuals who will feature in this book.

Geoffroi de Charny

De Charny was the most notable French knight of his generation, who wrote the standard work on knighthood, the *Book of Chivalry*. His military career began in 1337, the year when the current war between England and France began. He was captured by the English at Morlaix in 1342, and soon ransomed. He was knighted by 1343, and went on a futile crusade in 1345. De Charny did not fight at Crécy in 1346, but he played an increasingly important role in war after that. In 1349 he planned to regain Calais through bribery, but failed. Once again, the English took him prisoner, and he was again ransomed. He was one of the first members of the Order of the Star, and was chosen to carry the celebrated French war banner, the *Oriflamme*. In 1356 he was killed, banner in hand, fighting heroically at the battle of Poitiers. His *Book of Chivalry* was an attempt to renew and reform French knighthood, and sets out the ideals that a knight should follow.

John Hawkwood

An Essex man, Hawkwood's first military experience was in France, but the short-lived peace treaty agreed in 1360 meant he had to look elsewhere to continue his career. He found fame and a degree of fortune in Italy, initially with the mercenary band known as the White Company. He served Pisa, Milan, Padua, the Papacy, and above all Florence, whose authorities praised him to the skies. He was first hired by the Florentines in 1377, and fought for the city, with intermissions, until his death in 1394. Hawkwood was a soldier of immense ability, who understood the full complexities of war. Tactician, strategist and inspiring leader, he could turn apparent defeat into triumph, and had the diplomatic skill to succeed in the complex world of Italian city rivalries. Hawkwood always wanted to return to England, but he died in Italy, the most notable of the mercenaries, or *condottieri*, who served the Florentine republic.

Boucicaut

Jean II le Maingre was nicknamed, like his father before him, Boucicaut, in an allusion to a fishing net. No one is quite sure why. Born in 1366, his military career began at a very young age. He fought in the French triumph over the Flemings at Roosebeke in 1382, and then went on campaigns in Spain, the Baltic and the eastern Mediterranean. In 1391, despite his youth, he was appointed as one of the two marshals of France. He went on the crusading expedition of 1396 against the Turks in the Balkans, and was captured at Nicopolis that year. After his release he fought for the Byzantine emperor before he was appointed governor of Genoa in 1401. Although a great soldier, he was no politician, and in 1409 the Genoese ousted him. Boucicaut was captured at Agincourt in 1415, and is now a prisoner in England. His biography was written in 1409, to justify and explain his not-very-successful rule of Genoa; it is a classic description of a chivalric career, even though its hero emerges as a self-righteous prig.

The challenge

You have a great deal to learn if you want to be a successful knight. Geoffroi de Charny in his *Book of Chivalry* explains that knights should be bold and eager to commit themselves to deeds of arms and adventures. They will face difficult trials and many discomforts; terrors will beset them, and they may be defeated and captured. The French poet Christine de Pizan paints a similar picture. As she says, a knight should be wise and good, gracious, courteous, generous, gentle and calm. He should journey far to acquire honour, and should be enterprising and proud in undertaking deeds of arms. These are the ideals; to be really successful you need to add other, more practical elements, as well as a little low cunning.

Some skills are essential – you won't get very far if you don't know how to ride a horse, wield a lance and fight with sword and shield. Then the different techniques required for jousting and for fighting in battle need to be mastered. You will need to be physically fit for gruelling campaigns, which may take place under the hot Mediterranean sun or in the dark frozen days of a Baltic winter. There is much more than that, however; you need to understand the culture of chivalry, with all its ambiguities and contradictions. There is the glamour of the tournament, and the courtly culture with its love songs and romances, its dinners and dances. But you must be as comfortable on the battlefield as on the dancefloor, dealing with the brutal side of war, the ravaging of the land and the slaughter of civilians. And on top of all this there are also the business aspects to learn, particularly the ransoming of prisoners.

It may seem as though you have a daunting amount to learn, and it is true that you do, but with the expert guidance contained in this manual a glorious career as a knight awaits you. Follow this advice and you will not fail.

Note

Every effort has been made to make the advice in this manual as up-to-date as possible. All the views expressed represent the opinions and knowledge of the period from 1300 to 1415.

II

Upbringing & Training

*Practise knightly things and learn arts that help you and
grant you honour in war.*

HANKO DÖBRINGER, *FECHTBUCH*, 1389

‡　　‡　　‡

s a knight, you will be expected to display many qualities. Skill
in the use of arms is essential; you will also need to understand
how to behave in the right way and how to fit into the upper-
class world.

Child's play

Children's play is the first step in learning how to fight.

‡ Toy knights, made of pewter, make good playthings.

‡ Edward I gave his sons toy castles and a miniature
siege engine to play with.

‡ Richard II had miniature guns as a boy.

When Boucicaut was young and played with his friends, they would
pretend that their caps were helmets and their sticks swords. They imitated
sieges and played at battles. Boucicaut was a good child; Bertrand du
Guesclin, who would do so much to restore French prestige in the wars
with England, was not. During his upbringing in Brittany, he used to
recruit local boys for his gang, and organize mock tournaments with them,
until his father forbad it. After that, young Bertrand would go off to the
local village to pick fights. All his father could do was lock him up, not
realizing what valuable knightly skills his wayward son was developing.

In a noble household

You will probably be sent away for your education, to be brought up as a page in a noble household. Christine de Pizan, widowed at 25, packed her eldest son off to England, to the Earl of Salisbury's household. On the earl's death in 1397 she wrote a poem recommending the boy to the duke of Orleans: 'For this I beg, valiant and gracious prince, that it please you to take him into your service.'

In an aristocratic household there will be a master to look after the education of the boys. He will teach you how to look after military equipment, and all the skills needed to use it. You will pick up a lot from listening to the knights and squires, and watching what they do. As Geoffroi de Charny explains:

Christine de Pizan, French poet and author, with her son. She sent him to England to learn about weaponry and good manners.

*They like to hear and listen to men of prowess talk of military deeds,
and to see men-at-arms with their weapons and armour and
enjoy looking at fine mounts and chargers.*

A knight needs to be proficient with weapons, but you will also need to learn proper manners at court, such as how to wait at table. There are other aspects of noble culture to imbibe. Although the full details of heraldry can be left to heralds, it is important to learn how to recognize and describe coats of arms, and to memorize as many as possible. This is a vital means of distinguishing friend from foe in the heat of battle. Listening to the stories of knightly heroes of the past, such as the tales of Arthur and his knights, should inspire you. You should note, however, that Boucicaut would not want you to read such trivia, but would limit your reading to serious works on the history of Greece and Rome, and the lives of the saints.

Physical training

A good knight needs physical strength, stamina, a good eye and fine co-ordination. You need hard exercise to develop these. Boucicaut provides the best model. As a young man, he realized the importance of athleticism to a knight. His exercise regime included:

- ✝ Long-distance running so as to gain endurance.
- ✝ Jumping into the saddle of his horse from the ground.
- ✝ Lifting weights to strengthen his arms.

Among many other feats, he could:

- ✝ Do a somersault wearing full armour (but without a helmet).
- ✝ Climb the reverse side of a ladder hand over hand, not using his feet, armed with a steel breastplate.
- ✝ Without armour, he could do the same using just one hand (believe that if you can).

Boucicaut practised constantly with a lance and with other weapons. He was not a tall man, but he was an exceptional athlete. It was not just in military exercises that he excelled; off the battlefield he was also an extremely good tennis player.

Practice with lance and sword

The lance is a difficult weapon; it requires immense skill to hold the point steady and to aim it correctly. Before practising this on horseback, boys can try it seated on a small cart, pulled by their friends. Various targets can be used; the quintain is the best. This consists of a vertical post, with a horizontal beam swivelling on the top. On one end of this is a shield, which is the target. A weighted sack at the other end balances the shield, and if you get the hit wrong, or move too slowly, it will swing round and give you a good wallop. Endless practice is needed.

Practice is also needed with the sword; you should be familiar with it both as a single-handed and a double-handed weapon. A sword can:

✞ Deliver both slashing and thrusting blows.

✞ Be used in defence, to ward off an opponent's weapon.

It is important to practise using the sword on horseback; at the battle of Nicopolis it was by slashing to right and left with his sword that Boucicaut was able to drive his horse through the Turkish ranks. And don't forget that the hilt and pommel can be used to strike when fighting at close quarters.

For sword fighting on foot, learn the four basic guards that can be used, and their variants, with all the different types of thrusts and cuts. There are German books that set out fencing methods in a lot of detail. One such *Fechtbuch* explains that:

> *You should always look for the upper openings rather than*
> *the lower, and go over his hilt with strikes or thrusts*
> *artfully and quickly. For you have better reach over the*
> *hilt than under it, and you are also much safer in*
> *all your fencing.*

Swordplay is not an art intended for everyone; this is a skill exclusively for the military elite. Master Roger le Skirmisour kept a fencing school in London in the early 14th century, but he was convicted of 'enticing thither the sons of respectable persons, so as to waste and spend the property of their fathers and mothers upon bad practices: the result being that they themselves became bad men'. He should not have been teaching military skills to townspeople.

Riding

It is important that you should gain expertise in handling horses. You will ride with long stirrups and an upright body posture. You need to ride smoothly, with good control at all times; you and your horse should be as one. Control comes with proper use of the bit and your spurs; do not be too hard with these. You should aim to be like the Spanish knight, Pero Niño, of whom it is said that 'he knew all about horses; he sought for them, tended them and made much of them. In his time had no man in Castile so many good mounts; he rode them and trained them to his liking, some for war, some for parade and others for jousting.'

This late 14th-century bas-relief shows an Italian knight, with visor raised. Note his straight-legged riding style. He holds his reins in his left hand, leaving his right free for wielding his sword.

A hunting scene showing a king bringing down a stag, the most highly prized quarry. Hunting is excellent practice for knights, but you won't have to shoot from horseback in war.

Hunting

The hunt provides some excellent training for war, as well as being the main recreation activity for the upper classes. Geoffroi de Charny wrote that 'it befits all men of rank to enjoy the sport of hunting with hawk and hound.' Through hunting you will learn such things as:

✠ How to handle a horse.

✠ How to dissect a stag and distribute the portions according to the proper conventions.

✠ How to kill a boar or a stag with a spear, which will be useful experience when it comes to killing a man.

✠ How to use a bow and a crossbow. These are not weapons that a knight is likely to use in war, but it is nonetheless valuable to have some experience of handling them.

If you do not hunt, it is hard to see how you can win the respect of your comrades-in-arms. The unfortunate Edward II of England had no taste for the chase, but instead preferred menial occupations such as hedging and ditching along with low-born fellows. It is hardly surprising that such a man was totally unsuccessful in war, and ended up losing his throne and, ultimately, his life.

Reading and writing

It is rare to be sent to school, as Boucicaut was for a time, but a knight should still learn to read and write. War is not just a matter of riding confidently into battle. This is a bureaucratic age. There are muster rolls to be kept, writs to be read and acted upon, and agreements and contracts to be made. Of course, there are clerks to do these things, but it is important to be able to keep a check on them. You may be surprised that knights should be literate, but the English knight Thomas Gray even wrote a history, the *Scalacronica*, and Henry, Duke of Lancaster, a devotional treatise, the *Book of Holy Medicine*. You may even be able to cheer your companions up on campaign by reading to them, as the king of Scots, Robert Bruce, is said to have done with the romance of Fierabras, the 15-foot-tall son of the king of Spain, 'who was honourably beaten by the right doughty Oliver'.

Here are some books that all knights should read:

✠ The standard book on the art of war, *De Re Militari*, by the Roman author Vegetius, perhaps in the French translation produced by Christine de Pizan. There is no need, however, to go quite so far as Vegetius does in his recommendations for training. He suggests that, among other things, young men should learn to swim, but this is hardly a necessary accomplishment for a knight.

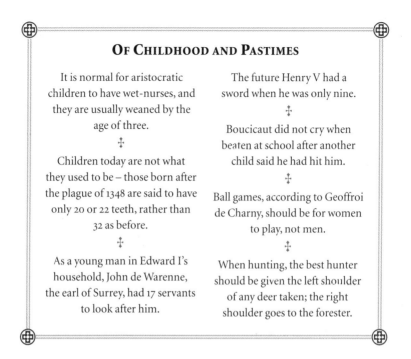

OF CHILDHOOD AND PASTIMES

It is normal for aristocratic children to have wet-nurses, and they are usually weaned by the age of three.

✝

Children today are not what they used to be – those born after the plague of 1348 are said to have only 20 or 22 teeth, rather than 32 as before.

✝

As a young man in Edward I's household, John de Warenne, the earl of Surrey, had 17 servants to look after him.

The future Henry V had a sword when he was only nine.

✝

Boucicaut did not cry when beaten at school after another child said he had hit him.

✝

Ball games, according to Geoffroi de Charny, should be for women to play, not men.

✝

When hunting, the best hunter should be given the left shoulder of any deer taken; the right shoulder goes to the forester.

✝ Geoffroi de Charny's *Book of Chivalry*.

✝ The Catalan polymath Ramon Llull's *Book of the Order of Chivalry*, which covers similar ground to de Charny's work, setting out the virtues a knight should ideally possess.

Go on campaign

The final stage of training is to acquire campaigning experience. Children can be taken to war at quite a young age as the following examples show:

✝ Edward III was only 14 when he rode in front of the troops on the 1327 Weardale campaign against the Scots.

✝ John of Gaunt, though at the age of ten he was far too young to bear arms, was present with his brother the Black Prince at the naval battle of Les Espagnols sur Mer in 1350.

✝ Boucicaut was 12 when he was taken on campaign in Normandy
in 1378. This was exceptionally young, and it's not surprising
that on his return he was taunted: 'Now look, master, there's
a fine man-at-arms! Get back to school!'

It is more usual for young men to acquire their first campaigning
experience and take up arms for the first time in their late teens.

The young squire

After you have been trained in the use of arms, you will not normally
become a knight straight away. You will first be a squire, perhaps like the
one described by the poet Geoffrey Chaucer in *The Canterbury Tales*. The
son of a knight, Chaucer's squire was about 20 years old, and had experience of the wars in France. Fashionably dressed, he could ride well, and
joust. He possessed the courtly skills; he could sing, dance, sketch and
write. This was a young man, much in love, who would surely soon receive
the accolade of knighthood.

The smartly-dressed squire from a manuscript of Geoffrey Chaucer's Canterbury Tales.
He told a romantic story set in far-off lands, but never reached the end.

Squires are equipped for war in much the same way as a knight, but are not expected to have such expensive armour or high-quality horses. Some people serve for many years as a squire before being knighted. Philip Chetwynd came of age in 1316, and was thinking about becoming a knight in 1319, when he entered the service of Ralph, Lord Basset of Drayton, but did not actually do so until 1339. Indeed, there are an increasing number of squires who never take the final step of being knighted.

What you will get out of it

Training is tough, but necessary. You will not be tested in the skills you have acquired in the use of weapons when you eventually become a knight; it will be taken for granted that you possess all the right abilities. Nor will you find that you are given training when on campaign; your commanders will assume that you are already competent and capable. As a result of your preparation you should:

- ✝ Be physically tough.
- ✝ Know how to manage your horse.
- ✝ Have expertise in wielding lance and sword.
- ✝ Have acquired courtly skills.

You will be ready to become a member of a military elite of the highest quality, and can hope to become a warrior of renown, a man of true prowess. As the chronicler Froissart explained:

> *Just as wood cannot burn without fire, neither can a noble man achieve perfect honour nor worldly glory without prowess.*

BECOMING A KNIGHT

*The order of chivalry is more exalted and noble than imagination
can suppose; and no knight ought to suffer himself to be debased
by cowardice, or any villainous or foul action; but when his
helmet is on his head he should be bold and fierce as a lion
when he sees his prey.*

KING JOÃO OF PORTUGAL, KNIGHTING MEN ON
THE EVE OF THE BATTLE OF ALJUBARROTA, 1385

✠   ✠   ✠

eing knighted is a major step for you. The ceremony itself is
an important rite of passage, which deserves to be taken
seriously. You will be taking on new responsibilities, and
accepting the dictates of the code of chivalry.

Who can become a knight?

Knighthood runs in families. If your father was a knight, then you in turn
should be able to become one. In France it is extremely difficult to become
a knight if you cannot show noble ancestry. Indeed, anyone who fights on
horseback with shield and lance has to have the right sort of lineage; a good
lineage will confer the right qualities and virtues on you. You also have to
be in a position to live without doing any kind of manual labour. It is
in theory possible to be ennobled by obtaining special royal *lettres
d'ennoblissement*, but these are very rarely issued. Nevertheless, it is possible in exceptional cases to rise in France from relatively obscure origins to
great heights, since performing on the battlefield with notable bravery
automatically ennobles a man.

✠ Bertrand du Guesclin came from a very minor Breton noble family; his military skills saw him become constable of France. He even acquired a ducal title in Spain and was offered the kingdom of Granada.

✠ Boucicaut's father came from an undistinguished family in Touraine, but rose in court service, displaying skill in diplomacy and war. He was appointed marshal of France in 1356.

The situation in Spain is similar to that in France. For Pero Niño, a knight of Castile, lineage was vitally important; he claimed descent from the royal dynasty of France on his father's side, and from one of the great noble houses of Castile on his mother's.

In England, theoretically, the situation should be much simpler, since everyone who possesses land worth £40 a year is supposed to become a knight. Regular orders are issued demanding that they do so or pay a fine instead. There, it is easier than in France for men of low or questionable birth to rise to knightly status, though you will not find a knight in trade, selecting and taking on an apprentice. Examples of men who have risen from obscure origins are:

✠ James Audley, a hero by any standards, was born illegitimate.

✠ Robert Knollys seems to have risen from Cheshire yeoman stock.

✠ John Hawkwood came from Essex; his father was a tanner who held a small amount of land. Gossip has it that as a boy John was apprenticed to a London tailor, though this is probably a malicious rumour.

✠ Robert Salle, who was killed by peasants in the revolt of 1382, is, ironically, said to have himself been born a villein, an unfree peasant.

In Germany, there are knightly families that were, in their distant origins, unfree. *Ministeriales* were officials who served the crown and the nobility, and rose to great heights in society in the 11th and 12th centuries despite the fact that they were not free. By the 14th century these origins had been forgotten, and all knights were considered noble, and hereditary. Social climbing is certainly frowned upon in Germany, however, as you can tell from the 13th-century poem about Helmbrecht, a peasant boy who became a robber-knight. He persuaded his sister to marry one of his gang, but at the wedding feast they were surprised and captured. Helmbrecht's followers were hanged; he was mutilated, and sometime later he was himself hanged by the peasants he had oppressed.

Italy is rather different, for here it is the great towns that dominate. As a result many knights are city dwellers, in contrast to the rest of Europe, where knights are more likely to be found on their country estates. In some places knighthood was bestowed rather too easily in the 12th and 13th centuries, on men not of true noble descent, and merchant wealth was translated into knightly and noble status. Now, however, that status is jealously guarded, but true knighthood is reserved only for those of noble lineage and a chivalric lifestyle. The Florentine poet Franco Sacchetti commented sarcastically on the idea of merchants becoming knights: 'If this type of knighthood is valid one might as well knight an ox or an ass – or any sort of beast.'

A small elite

Being a knight is a costly occupation, and many families that have been of knightly standing in the past can no longer afford the expense of knighthood. In England, where there had been perhaps 4,000 or more knights at the start of the 13th century, numbers dwindled to less than half that over the next hundred years. Knights are very much the elite among the cavalry both in England and France.

- ✝ In France by the middle of the 14th century the number of active knights was probably under 3,700. There, less than 12 per cent of the cavalry are knights; over 87 per cent are squires or plain men-at-arms.

- ✝ In England the proportion of knights was rather higher; almost a quarter of the cavalry in the Black Prince's force on the 1359 campaign in France were of knightly rank. After that, numbers fell, and by the time of the battle of Agincourt, only about 8 per cent of the cavalry were knights.

Increasingly, people are satisfied with the status of a squire, which has become ever more formalized. Squires, for example, can bear coats of arms. Richard II gave permission to John de Kingston to do this when a French knight challenged him:

> *We have received him in the estate of gentleman, and have made him a squire, and wish that he should be known by his arms which he shall bear in future, that is to say, of argent with an azure hat and ostrich feather, gules.*

Although squires are going up in the world, there is no doubt that the knights are the true elite in society and in war, and it is to knighthood that you should aspire.

Look the part

It probably helps if you look right. Boucicaut was not tall, but he was good looking, and according to his biographer he had a splendid physique. His chest was broad, his shoulders sloping and well shaped. His limbs were ideally formed. His hair was brown, as was his beard. His look was assured and wise. However, you should not worry too much if you don't match up to such a description. Bertrand du Guesclin was emphatically not an ideal knight in appearance. He was small, dark and ugly, but his achievements were remarkable.

If you are too fat, or have a physical deformity, the theorist Ramon Llull tells us that you cannot become a knight. You can certainly use an abnormality as a convenient excuse if you do not want the promotion. In 1346 John of Bella Aqua was pardoned for disobeying King Edward III of England's instructions that he take up knighthood, because he had a malformed right foot.

BERTRAND DU GUESCLIN

A Breton, from the minor nobility, du Guesclin was knighted in 1354. He distinguished himself in the defence of Rennes, 1356–57, but was defeated at Auray in 1364; he later fought in Spain, and in 1367 was defeated at Nájera. Du Guesclin developed tactics for dealing with the English, and his main successes came after hostilities between England and France were renewed in 1369, when he re-conquered many territories for the French king. He was appointed constable of France in 1370, and died in 1380.

The ceremony of knighthood

As a would-be knight, you will have been a squire for some time, gaining valuable experience. There is no fixed age at which you should become a knight; that depends on your own wishes, and whether you can afford the costs involved. If you are lucky, you may find that some of the expenses are born by your lord. What becoming a knight means above all is that you accept the obligations inherent in the chivalric code: you should bear arms in a just cause, fighting for the Church, for your lord, or for your lineage. As Geoffroi de Charny explained:

> *And for those who perform deeds of arms more to gain God's grace and for the salvation of the soul than for glory in this world, their noble souls will be set in paradise to all eternity.*

In his book, de Charny described the classic full knighting ceremony. It begins with your confessing, and repenting of all your sins.

Receiving the belt of knighthood, as shown in this early 14th-century manuscript, is a key part of the knighting ceremony. The belt is actually more important as a symbol than the sword.

1 On the day before the actual knighting, you take a bath, and stay in it for a long time; you probably don't have baths very often, and may find this a bit off-putting, but it is necessary. The idea is not that you should become physically clean, though that may be an unintended consequence. The bath is symbolic; in it you will be cleansed of your sins and get rid of all the impurities of your past life.

2 You will come out of the water a new man, and must then go and rest on a new bed with clean linen; it should be as if you have emerged from a great fight against sin and the Devil.

3 When you get up, knights come to help you to dress for the ceremony. A red tunic symbolizes your readiness to shed blood in defending the faith, and black stockings remind you of your mortality. A white belt symbolizes purity and chastity, and a red cloak is worn to show humility. Then, you go to church for a long vigil.

4 The ceremony itself on the next day is preceded by a mass. After this mass:

- ✝ Knights fix gilded spurs to your boots.
- ✝ You are given the belt that is an important emblem of knighthood.
- ✝ The man who is to confer the honour of knighthood on you then hands over a sword, kisses you, and taps you on the shoulder.

There is a great deal of solemn ritual and symbolism in the ceremony, but despite all the religious elements, the conferring of knighthood is not actually done by the Church, unlike the coronation of a king. Knighthood is a secular rank, and should be awarded by men who have themselves shown distinction as knights.

Knighting ceremonies can take place on a very large scale. In England, in 1306, some 300 men were knighted along with the king's son, the future Edward II. The new knights were all given cloth to make their mantles, along with a mattress and a quilt. A receipt provides the details:

> *I, William Beler, have received from Master Thomas of Usflete,*
> *Clerk of the King's Great Wardrobe, for the use of Henry le*
> *Vavasseur, for making him a new knight, by order of the lord King*
> *by privy seal, namely, for his* cointesia, *6 ells of cloth of Tarsus*
> *and one* pena *of squirrel fur of 8 rows. For his cape during vigil,*
> *4 ells of brown mixed cloth. For his two robes, 10½ ells of green*
> *and 10½ ells of azure blue cloth, 2 furs of 'popple' and 2 furs of*
> *squirrel, each of 6 rows, and 2 hoods of marten fur of 4 rows.*
> *Item, for his bed, that is for his quilt, 2 lengths of cloth of*
> *gold in Meseneaux and one piece of worsted, 24 ells,*
> *and for that of his canvas, 10 ells.*

For some of the 300 knights-to-be, the vigil took place in Westminster Abbey, but it was not the solemn occasion it should have been. The great church was surrounded by a cheerful mob, and there was a tremendous din with shouting and trumpet playing. Some of the aspirant knights went to other churches, such as the Temple, only to find them overcrowded. The ceremony itself in the abbey was a disaster, for two knights were crushed to death near the great altar, and others fainted in the throng as they tried to move forward to be dubbed. Despite the tragedy, a great feast was held to mark the occasion. Two gilded swans formed a centrepiece, on which the new knights swore a range of oaths. A hundred or so minstrels provided entertainment.

Knighting before battle

Don't worry if you find the elaborate initiation rite of knighthood off-putting; there are easier ways to gain the honour. It is customary for commanders to knight some of their followers on the eve of battle, and this is done in a very simple ceremony, demanding nothing more than an oath and a tap on the shoulder.

- ✠ Edward III knighted the Black Prince and a number of others just as the English were about to land in Normandy in 1346.

- ✠ In 1367 in Spain many in the English army were knighted when battle was imminent. John Chandos's herald explained that:
  The prince knighted king Pedro first of all, then Thomas Holland, Hugh, Philip and Peter Courtenay; John Trivet and Nicholas Bond. The duke knighted Ralph Camoys, Walter Ursewick, Thomas d'Auvirmetri and John Grendon; he made twelve or so knights in all.

- ✠ The young Boucicaut was knighted by the duke of Bourbon just before the battle of Roosebeke in 1382.

In 1385, before the battle of Aljubarrota, the king of Portugal issued a proclamation, asking anyone who wanted to become a knight to come forward. About 60 did so; but for some reason none of the English in the army were prepared to accept the king's invitation. Perhaps they did not like the idea of being knighted by a foreigner.

These pre-battle knighting ceremonies do not always go well. There was some embarrassment when the English and French armies faced each other at Buirenfosse in 1339. No engagement took place, as neither side was convinced of the prospects of success in battle. The armies, however, were fully prepared to fight, and there was a long, tedious wait to see if any action would take place. Then a hare ran across the fields between the two hosts; both sides shouted and cheered as they saw it. Some, however, mistook the shouting for the start of battle, and knighted their followers, who, poor chaps, were always thereafter known as the Knights of the Hare.

The coat of arms

Coats of arms are extremely important. They are not just a method of identification; they carry with them messages about a man's lineage and his connections in society. You are unlikely to have to acquire a brand-new coat of arms, as your father will almost certainly have one. You just need to modify his slightly, by means of what is known as a label, a horizontal strip.

✠ Be careful not to have the same coat of arms as someone else.

✠ In 1300 there was little more than surprise when Brian FitzAlan and Hugh Poinz were both found to carry the same banner, but such problems have become much more serious since then.

✠ Before the battle of Poitiers in 1356 John Chandos encountered a French marshal, Jean de Clermont. Both bore a badge of a lady in blue, with a sunbeam. Clermont had the last word, condemning the English: 'You never think of anything new yourselves, but when you see something good, you just take it.'

✠ There was a famous case in the English court of chivalry between Richard le Scrope and Robert Grosvenor in 1386, for the two men had discovered that they bore the same coat of arms, *azur a bend or*. The eventual outcome favoured Scrope.

This heraldic roll of about 1280 displays the coats of arms of almost 700 knights. Heralds produce rolls such as this to provide a record of the designs and symbols that knights use to identify themselves, helping to avoid embarrassing and dangerous mix-ups.

So, make sure that your own coat of arms really is unique. If you are in a position to choose your own, you might try a pun on your name; Hugh Calveley, for example, bore three calves on his coat of arms, while Robert de Scales used silver shells as his symbol.

A provision in Ralph, Lord Basset of Drayton's will shows the importance of the family name and coat of arms (as well as of his bed):

> *I will that the person, whosoever he be, that shall first bear my surname and arms, according to my will, shall have the use of my great velvet bed for life, but it is not to be given away from him who should bear my name and arms.*

The world of chivalry

You will be familiar with the concepts of chivalry before you become a knight; in his book Geoffroi de Charny expects men-at-arms and knights to share the same values. Nonetheless, the process of knighting can be seen as marking your formal entry into the chivalric world.

The chivalric ideals are:

✝ *largesse*, or generosity   ✝ *courtoisie*, or courtesy

✝ *prouesse*, or prowess   ✝ *loyauté*, or loyalty

As Chandos's herald wrote of the Black Prince:

The noble prince of whom I speak never, from the day of his birth, thought of anything but loyalty, noble deeds, valour and goodness, and was endowed with prowess.

These are not new ideas; they date back at least as far as the 12th century, and underlying them is a mixture of Christianity and warrior ethos. Chivalry is not a code for all; it is exclusive, limited to those of the right status in society. Peasants and townspeople have little understanding of it, so you can treat them however you like.

THE BLACK PRINCE

The eldest son of Edward III of England, the Black Prince distinguished himself at Crécy in 1346, led a raid from Gascony to the Mediterranean in 1355, and in 1356 was victorious at Poitiers. Later he went to Spain on campaign, winning the battle of Nájera in 1367. His sack of Limoges in 1370 was brutal, and became notorious. A few years later illness struck him, and he died in 1376, a year before his father.

OF KNIGHTING

Five thousand eels, 287 cod, 136 pike and 102 salmon were among the supplies collected for the feast held in 1306 when the future Edward II was knighted.

✠

It is said that the earl of Gloucester was killed at Bannockburn in 1314 because he was not wearing his coat of arms, and so could not be recognized.

✠

John Hawkwood was a knight, but it is not known where or when he was knighted.

Geoffroi de Charny suggested that any knight who failed to make a name for himself should have his teeth pulled out, one by one.

✠

Four hundred and sixty-seven new knights were created immediately before the battle of Roosebeke in 1382.

✠

Kings were entitled to collect a tax from their subjects, and lords money from their tenants, when an eldest son was knighted.

Chivalry is an international code; knights throughout the Christian world share its values. Stories from romance, familiar across Europe, provide part of the cultural background. You will find that Italians are quite as knowledgeable as Englishmen about King Arthur and his knights. Although this is a time of a growing sense of national identity, this can be overridden by allegiance to the knightly world of international chivalry. You will find that knights have considerable respect for each other, even if they are on opposing sides in war.

Further promotion

Once you have become a knight, you can be promoted further, to the rank of banneret. This means that you will bear a square or rectangular banner, rather than a long pennon as your standard, and in war you will have command of a much larger troop than you would as a knight. This is a purely military promotion; being a banneret does not have implications for your social standing. Nor does it carry with it the kind of chivalric baggage about honour and prowess that is implied in becoming a knight.

Froissart tells the story of John Chandos' promotion. Before the battle of Nájera in 1367, John presented his banner to the Black Prince, saying that he now possessed sufficient lands to warrant his promotion. The prince duly cut off the tail of the banner, so as to make it square, and returned it to John. The process was a simple one, but to deserve his elevation Chandos had not only distinguished himself in war, but also demonstrated that he had the wealth to maintain his new position. So, you should not expect to become a banneret for many years.

There are two high military offices that you can aspire to, those of marshal and constable. It helps if these run in the family:

✦ Boucicaut was promoted to marshal, and the fact that his father had held the post was one of the reasons.

✦ Bertrand du Guesclin's appointment as constable was purely on merit.

These are not purely honorific titles. The two marshals and the constable of France have their courts; the marshals in particular claim wide jurisdiction over military matters. There are rights that go with these offices; the constable, for example, has a claim to all horses and harness taken when a castle or fortress is captured.

What to aim for

You need to think about all the chivalric values, but you will find that they do not always coincide with the realities that you face. By all means display *largesse*, and be generous; but remember that you have to make money to maintain your position. Be courteous and gracious, but show that you are tough and determined when necessary. You will find that your reputation depends above all on your display of prowess. Show that you are bold, brave and skilful in the use of arms; that is the mark of a true knight.

Arms, Armour & Horses

Their armour was almost uniformly a cuirass and a steel breastplate,
iron arm-pieces, thigh- and leg-pieces; they carried stout daggers
and swords; all had tilting lances which they dismounted to use.

FILIPPO VILLANI, *CHRONICLE*, 1364

✠   ✠   ✠

t is essential to be provided with proper protection, both for
fighting in battles and sieges, and for tournaments. You will
not be able to manage with just one set of equipment for all
purposes; armour is becoming increasingly specialized. You
would find yourself seriously limited in what you could do if you tried
wearing tournament armour in battle. You will need a range of weapons,
the main ones being the lance and sword. A good knight must also have
good horses; indeed, your warhorse will be your main item of expenditure.

Mail, leather and plate armour

Several materials can be used to make armour.

✠ Mail, made of interlinked riveted rings, is a key component.
  It resists cuts well but, being flexible, does not help to defend
  against crushing blows.

✠ Plate, made of metal sheets, can resist both cutting and
  crushing blows.

✠ *Cuir bouilli* is hardened leather; it is relatively light and strong.

✠ Baleen, plates of whalebone, is another very useful material,
  which is often used for tournament armour.

Armour has changed a lot over the past century. Old-fashioned mail has been increasingly abandoned in favour of steel plate. The chronicler Jean le Bel, a Hainaulter, remarked that when he went to England in 1327, the English knew nothing of plate armour, but wore long tunics, or hauberks, of mail, with surcoats bearing their coats of arms, and great helmets of iron or *cuir bouilli*. Within a little more than a decade, they were wearing modern plate. Jean was exaggerating; plate was already known in 13th-century England, but the start of the French war in 1337 certainly helped to bring the English up to date. As a well-equipped knight, nowadays, fortunately, you will be fully encased in a carefully constructed and ingeniously jointed suit of plate armour.

Plate armour is cleverly constructed so as to provide not only strength, but also as much movement as possible, as the joints on this steel gauntlet show.

Where should you buy armour?

You will do best to go direct to an armourer; that way you can be sure of a good fit. Alternatively, there are some retail outlets in big cities that sell armour; Francesco Datini, an Italian merchant from Prato, had a shop in Avignon for a time, which was useful for knights fighting in the war between England and France. The best armour is made in Italy, in Milan; there are also excellent armourers in Germany, where Cologne is a major centre of production.

The helmet

The most important thing to protect is your head. You need cloth padding first of all, to protect you from the chafing of the mail coif, or headpiece, that you wear under your helmet.

RIGHT *A complete suit of armour, made in Milan at the end of the last century. The breastplate is covered in velvet; the body and limbs are completely protected by steel plate. The helmet is a bacinet, with a cone-shaped visor; a mail avantail protects the neck and shoulders.*

OPPOSITE *This 14th-century great helm has no movable visor, and is more suitable for use in tournaments than in battle.*

The great helm

The type of old-fashioned helmet known as a great helm is a massive piece of equipment that rests on your shoulders; it probably has a grand crest mounted on top of it. It has slits to see through, which also serve for very necessary ventilation – you will get very hot wearing one of these. There is no movable visor, and with these helmets, the best advice is to not put it on until absolutely necessary. Back in the 13th century the great helm had a flat top, which made it easy to manufacture, but offered little protection to a blow from a mace or war hammer.

The tournament helmet

The kind of helmet now used in tournaments developed from the great helm. The flat top has been replaced by a more conical shape, which deflects blows better. The very latest form of tournament helmet could be

---

TECHNOLOGY

Improvements in manufacturing methods have made the recent changes to armour possible; for example, the use of hammers powered by water mills has mechanized part of the production process, while water-powered bellows can increase the temperature for smelting. Wrought iron can be bent quite easily; it does not have the rigidity needed for good armour, and certainly would be no use for a sword. Steel is produced if a small amount of carbon is added to the iron. It is possible by a complex process of heating and cooling the metal to temper it, and to control the degree of hardness; in this way an expert armourer can ensure that the outer surfaces of a piece of metal are hard, while the inner retains the malleability than means it does not shatter. Armourers have a number of anvils of different shapes, as well as special hammers, for forming the various different pieces of armour, which then need to be polished and finished.

---

termed 'frog-mouthed'. It has a projecting curved lip below the eye-slits, so that when you sit upright or lean back your face is fully protected.

When you put your tournament helmet on, tie the laces at the back first. The laces should not be too strong; a blow in the right place should be capable of knocking your helmet right off. Curiously, this is safer than having the helmet fixed immovably, but you will still get a fearful wrench to your neck.

The bacinet

You could wear a helmet of the great helm type in battle, but the fact that you cannot see much, or even breathe properly, is a bit of a drawback. The bacinet is far more practical. At the start of the 14th century this was little more than a steel skull cap, which you could even wear under a great helm. Then a movable visor was added, which could be fixed in a raised position until combat began. This way you could see and hear what was going on, but still have proper protection. Your neck would be protected by a piece of mail. Modern bacinets may seem rather odd, for the visor is normally conical in shape, making you look rather like a dog, or even a pig. Yet this shape is very practical. It leaves enough air in front of your face so you can breathe, and you are not likely to get a broken nose from hitting your head against the visor. At the battle of Nogent-sur-Seine in 1359, Eustace d'Auberchicourt commanded the English forces. One of the French managed to hurl his lance at Eustace. It hit him on the visor and penetrated it. Eustace suffered three broken teeth, but he was still able to continue the fight; the visor had taken most of the force of the blow.

You may think that you will look odd in this Italian bacinet with its snout-shaped visor, but no one will laugh at you. The visor offers excellent protection, and enables you to breathe easily.

Body protection

Your upper body can be protected in various ways. You can have:

- ✝ A padded jacket, known as a gambeson, or aketon, under your armour. The English knight John FitzMarmaduke had a very stylish red aketon, with sleeves made of baleen.

- ✝ A 'pair of plates' – strips of overlapping steel plate fixed to a cloth or leather jacket; an advance on the mail hauberk. Plates often look best covered with grand cloth. When the French attacked Rye on the English south coast in 1377, they were impressed by an Englishman they captured, for his coat of plates was covered with gold velvet.

- ✝ A cuirass, or solid breastplate, is up to date, and is particularly suitable for jousting.

- ✝ *Aillettes* on your shoulders are protective pieces with a decorative purpose, in that they bear your coat of arms. These, however, went out of fashion around 1350.

The best protection for the arms and legs is provided by pieces of plate for thighs and shins, with knee-pieces. Armoured footwear is also needed.

Some changes in armour are dictated by fashion; early in the 14th century a flowing surcoat was the thing to wear over your armour, but that has been replaced by the fitted jupon, which is far smarter in every way.

All this armour sounds like a very heavy weight to carry. In fact, it is not too bad. Because the weight is well distributed over the body, you will find that plate armour is easier to wear than an old-fashioned mail hauberk. You should certainly be able to mount your horse, wearing full armour, without needing to ask for help.

Getting it on

It is quite a business to put your armour on, and you will certainly need some help from an attendant. There are many different parts, and you need to make sure that each is well secured.

NAMING OF PARTS

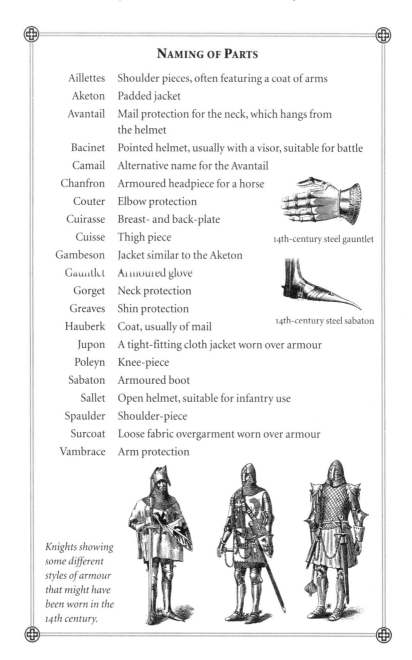

Aillettes Shoulder pieces, often featuring a coat of arms

Aketon Padded jacket

Avantail Mail protection for the neck, which hangs from the helmet

Bacinet Pointed helmet, usually with a visor, suitable for battle

Camail Alternative name for the Avantail

Chanfron Armoured headpiece for a horse

Couter Elbow protection

Cuirasse Breast- and back-plate

Cuisse Thigh piece

14th-century steel gauntlet

Gambeson Jacket similar to the Aketon

Gauntlet Armoured glove

Gorget Neck protection

Greaves Shin protection

Hauberk Coat, usually of mail

14th-century steel sabaton

Jupon A tight-fitting cloth jacket worn over armour

Poleyn Knee-piece

Sabaton Armoured boot

Sallet Open helmet, suitable for infantry use

Spaulder Shoulder-piece

Surcoat Loose fabric overgarment worn over armour

Vambrace Arm protection

Knights showing some different styles of armour that might have been worn in the 14th century.

It can be a real struggle to get into your armour. You will need a servant to fasten the buckles and tie all the laces. Give yourself plenty of time.

This is how armour was put on for a tournament in the early 14th century. Of course, nowadays you would probably be fully equipped with plate armour and bacinet, rather than wearing a mail hauberk and great helm.

- ✝ First of all, light a fire in the room where you are to get ready; you don't want to freeze. There should be a carpet on the floor.

- ✝ Then strip to your shirt and comb your hair.

- ✝ Start with the feet, and put on leather shoes.

- ✝ Put on greaves for your shins, which may be of steel, or *cuir bouilli*. Thigh and knee protectors follow.

- ✝ Then put on a padded coat, or aketon, followed by a shirt and coif.

- ✝ A skull-piece comes next.

- ✝ A mail hauberk follows, with leather protection on top.

- ✝ Over all this goes a surcoat, which bears your coat of arms.

- ✝ Gauntlets follow, and finally, you don the great helm.

Maintenance

Keeping your armour in good condition is not easy, for even the best-quality steel rusts. Paint or gilding will help, of course. Plate armour can be polished fairly easily, though it's hard work, but it's more difficult to keep mail bright. One way is to use a barrel of bran. Put your armour in it, and roll it about. The bran polishes the armour, and the oil in it will protect it to some extent from rust.

Cost

Armour is not cheap. An inventory of an elderly English knight's possessions made in 1374 gives some comparative prices, which show that it takes about 14 day's wages to buy a bacinet (wages being around 2 shillings a day). It also demonstrates how relatively expensive it is to equip a horse properly.

Bacinet with aventail	£1 6s. 8d.
Saddle and horse armour	£6 6s. 8d.
Three hauberks	£8 13s. 4d.
Two pairs of plate gauntlets	6s. 8d.

This is what some Spanish armour came to in 1383; the most expensive item is the coat of mail, which took a lot of labour to make:

Bacinet with aventail	20 florins
Coat of mail	25 florins
A piece of iron	15 florins
Harness of leg pieces	10 florins
Gauntlets	4 florins

Naturally, armour merchants are doing rather well during the current period of war across Europe. In his shop in Avignon in 1367 Francesco Datini had the following for sale:

45 bacinets	60 breastplates	23 pairs of gauntlets
3 iron hats	20 cuirasses	
10 skullcaps	12 coats of mail	

Horses

It is impossible to envisage a knight without his horse. As the French legal expert Honoré Bouvet has it: 'A knight is bold, too, by reason of his horse in which he has complete trust.' In fact, you will need at least two horses for yourself, with more for your followers. There are several different sorts of horse:

- ✝ The destrier, the charger, is the grandest horse. These are large and powerful, probably up to 16 hands in height. If you have one of these, you will probably choose not to ride it much, but will keep it in reserve for use in battle.

- ✝ The courser, a lighter horse, is easy to ride and effective in war and tournament.

- ✝ The palfrey is a riding horse, with a distinctive smooth gait.

- ✝ Hackneys are also useful as riding horses.

- ✝ Rouncey is a rather old-fashioned term for ordinary horses.

It is important that your horse is well dressed. The knight's horse shown here is fully covered or 'barded'.

For fighting, you should aim to have a destrier or a courser. The best horses come from Spain or Italy, but horse-trading is big business, and you can even find, for example, Hungarian horses sold as far afield as England. A top-class destrier may cost £100 or even more; it is hard to find one for less than £40 or £50. Only those of the highest rank can afford such splendid animals. At the other end of the spectrum, it is possible to find an adequate horse for £5, and a pack animal for less than that.

KNIGHTS DO IT ON HORSEBACK

The very name of chivalry is connected to the horse, *cheval* in French, and Thomas Gray the elder once remarked that if you wanted to do a chivalrous deed, then you should be on horseback. King Pedro IV of Aragon wrote that he was much better at fighting on horseback than on foot. In the poem *Sir Launfal*, the hero made a fool of himself when he failed to manage his horse.

> *He rode with little pride*
> *His horse slipped and slid in the fen*
> *Wherefore scorned him many men*
> *About him far and wide.*

Your horse is part of your identity as a knight. Yet, ironically, you will discover that in most circumstances the best way to fight is to dismount and face the enemy on foot.

Horses come in a wide range of colours, but the majority are bay, chestnut or black, with some greys. There is no particular prestige involved; the colour does not reflect the quality of the animal.

You need to give your horse a name. Bayard is a safe bet, particularly for a bay; many horses are called this, with the addition of some further identifier such as a family name. Bayard, of course, was the heroic magic horse who features in many romances. Morel is a good name for a dark brown horse, again with a family name added as in Morel de Mohaut, or a place name, as with Morel de Durham.

Your expensive horse needs protection; think of him in battle, with arrows hissing their way towards you. The minimum you need is a chanfron to protect his head, but you can also equip him properly with a cover of mail, worn over a good layer of padding. Over it all is a cloth cover, which will bear your coat of arms. This is an important piece of equipment; there is a clear distinction in the field between those fully armed cavalrymen who ride what are known as covered, or barded, horses, and others such as archers whose mounts appear bare.

Saddles are important too. These have a high pommel and cantle, which may almost wrap round the rider, particularly in the case of saddles designed for jousting. This way you are held securely in the saddle, so as help to withstand any blows; a hit from a lance is unlikely to push you off. Stirrups are long, so that your legs will be almost straight as you sit; this means that you will be in a solid position to fight with lance or sword.

Horses need a good deal of looking after. A destrier in particular eats a great deal, and you should allocate half a bushel (15 lb) of oats a day for one. A more ordinary horse needs half as much. In addition, horses need hay, until the summer months when they can be put to graze in the fields. They also need shoeing regularly, and it is necessary to ensure a regular supply of nails and horseshoes. Girths, halters and other harnessing equipment are required. Should your horse not be on top form, don't despair, as there are lots of medicines for horses. Wine can be used, and vinegar. Dragon's blood, frankincense, fenugreek, turpentine, and olive oil also feature in lists of horse cures.

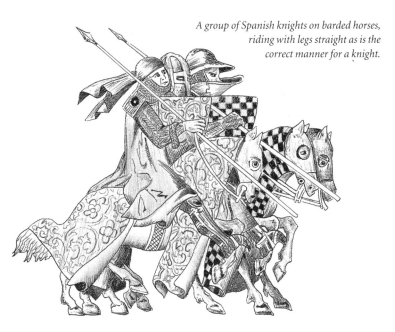

A group of Spanish knights on barded horses, riding with legs straight as is the correct manner for a knight.

Shields

Shields used to be long and kite-shaped, but by the early 14th century they had changed a great deal. They became quite small, triangular in shape, with a flat rather than a curved surface. Shields are normally made of wood and leather, and of course bear a coat of arms. They are an important part of tournament equipment; they may have a cut-out in the top right corner into which the lance can be slotted. For war, however, you will probably prefer not to carry a shield. Infantry troops will use shields, either rectangular *targes*, or small circular bucklers, but the fully armoured knight has little need of one, whether fighting on horseback or on foot.

Lances

The lance is an impressive weapon, up to 14 feet in length, normally made from ash, and often grandly painted. Just think of the full weight of man and horse, and the impetus behind the charge, all concentrated on the single point of the lance. The force is immense. The lance is not to be thrown, like a javelin; it relies on the momentum of man and horse. As you ride, the lance is carried vertically, on a rest fixed to the saddle; it is then lowered and

LEFT *A jousting lance, with its blunt coronal, and to its left a war lance, with a pointed steel tip.*

OPPOSITE *Swords vary in type, but most have a central ridge to provide strength, a cross-piece for protection, and a pommel.*

couched for the charge. You hold the lance fairly close to the butt end, under your arm, and normally angle it across your horse's neck, so that the point is on the animal's left. The lance is thicker at the butt end, so weighting it, but even so, it is not a well-balanced weapon, and you will need a good deal of strength to hold it up and aim it effectively.

For jousting, a more specialized lance is needed. Rather than having a sharp point, it will have a blunt end, called a coronal, which looks a little like a crown with three little projections on it. There will also be a vamplate, or hand-guard. It is good in a joust to break your lance with a decent blow to your opponent, so the lance does not need to be too strong, though it should only shatter from a true hit. Your breastplate should be fitted with an *arret*, or lance-stop, so that the lance can be rested on it, or even slotted into place with a piece on the lance called a grate; this ensures that all your weight, and that of your horse, is behind the blow you strike. You need a good many lances, to replace all those you hope to break, for a broken lance is a point in your favour in a joust.

Swords

The sword is a truly noble weapon, the two cutting edges symbolizing the knight's duty 'to defend right, reason and justice on all sides without being false to the Christian faith', as Geoffroi de Charny puts it. There are many different types of sword, but the basic characteristics are that they have a long, two-sided blade, with a cross-piece and pommel for the hilt. The pommel can be simple and round, but a decorative shape may be more fashionable. The sword is normally stiffened by means of a ridge running down the centre.

A sword may look simple, but it is a complex weapon to make. The smith must forge it from a billet of metal; when heated so that it becomes malleable, it is hammered into shape. A modern sword is normally made from a single piece of steel; the days are gone when swords were made from several rods of iron, twisted and folded as they were forged into a single blade. Careful heating and cooling is used to temper the blade. The sword is useless if it is brittle; equally it is of little value in fighting if it is soft and bends easily.

- ✝ The art of the smith is to give the blade both strength and hardness.

- ✝ Balance is important in a sword; the way that it tapers towards the tip is important in weighting the blade towards the hilt.

- ✝ A good sword should not be too heavy; about 3 lb is probably the ideal weight.

Swords are changing as a result of the development of plate armour; older weapons have a broad blade suitable for slashing or cutting, newer ones are stiff and more tapered, with a sharp point designed for thrusting.

There are alternatives to the sword.

- ✝ The falchion is a broad-bladed, curved weapon with a single cutting edge, a good deal shorter than a sword, but nonetheless effective at delivering a slashing blow.

- ✝ The mace is a heavy club; the chronicler Froissart described a knight in 1373 who had one made of lead 'with which he smashed every helmet that came within reach of it', but he himself was hit on the head in retaliation, a blow he never fully recovered from. Similar to the mace is the war hammer.

- ✝ The axe is another useful weapon. Remember the way in which Robert Bruce dealt with Henry de Bohun in the build-up to the battle of Bannockburn, cleaving his head in two with his axe and breaking its handle. Bertrand du Guesclin's favourite weapon was the axe, and Boucicaut had an axe knocked from his hand at the battle of Roosebeke.

RIGHT *Crossbows are slow to load, but are highly effective in siege warfare. Here a one-foot crossbow is being spanned and shot.*

OPPOSITE *A battleaxe is an extremely deadly weapon. This one has both a blade for slashing and a penetrating point.*

Other weapons

There are many other weapons used in war; as a knight it is important to understand what they can do and how they operate, but you do not require skills in their use.

The crossbow is an infantry weapon.

✝ A one-foot crossbow is held down with a single stirrup for loading.

✝ A two-feet crossbow is held down with both feet for loading.

✝ A crossbow *à tour* is loaded with a winch.

The crossbow shoots a fearsome heavy bolt. It is much used in the defence of castles, and on the battlefield crossbowmen equipped with massive shields, or *pavises*, are to be feared. The problem with the crossbow is that it is slow; reloading it is laborious.

The bow is a much simpler weapon, but one which requires a lot of skill and strength from the user.

✝ The English use longbows. Ideally made of yew, and some 6 feet or more in length, it is possible to shoot with them at a far faster rate than with a crossbow. The longbow has an effective range of at least 200 yards. The hail of arrows from a body of English archers is frightening indeed; this can be a devastating weapon against cavalry.

✠ The Saracens use much shorter bows of a very different type. These are not made from a single piece of wood, but are composite, often made from layers of wood and horn glued together, and shaped in an ingenious curve. The storm of Turkish arrows is just as frightening as that from the English longbows.

Pole weapons are worryingly effective against knightly cavalry, and you should not think that because they look simple they can do no harm.

✠ Steel pikes from Bordeaux are highly regarded weapons.

✠ Simple spears in the hands of the Scots, formed up in the tight formation known as the

LEFT *The longbow, 6 feet or more in length, requires great strength to draw. The best bows are made from Iberian yew, and may have a draw-weight of 150 lbs or more.*

OPPOSITE *Pole axes or halberds vary in type. All are highly effective in the hands of infantry troops.*

OF ARMOUR

The total weight of armour should be no more than about 50 or 60 lbs.

✠

You can be suffocated in a suit of armour in very hot weather.

✠

At the battle of Auray, Hugh Calveley and his men took off their leg armour, so as to gain mobility.

Armour won't protect you entirely: William Despenser was killed in 1337 when an arrow went through three layers of mail and three folds of his aketon.

✠

Edward III took his smith, Andrew le Fevre, with him on the 1346 campaign; Andrew's mother was left to carry on her son's work at the Tower of London.

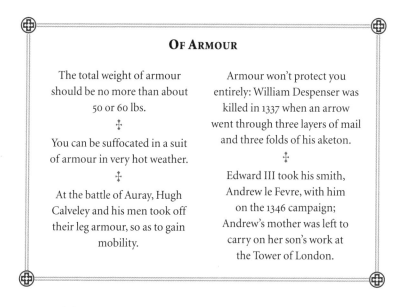

schiltrom, are quite enough to hold off a determined charge.

✠ Halberds, poles with a cutting and thrusting blade fixed to the end, are frightening. The Swiss are particularly adept at using these to see off German cavalry.

There are also great machines used in siege warfare, huge stone-throwing engines, guns and other types of weapon. These are not for knights to use; there are expert engineers and gunners who know how to operate them. You do need to understand their capabilities, however, and these will be explained in chapter 12.

‡ V ‡

ORDERS OF KNIGHTHOOD

And at this feast he ordained a thing new and unused by the crown, choosing sixty of the barons and knights, who swore faith and company together with the said king, under a certain order of their life, and of their activities and vestments ... And it was called the Company of the Knot.

MATTEO VILLANI, *CHRONICLE*, 1352

‡   ‡   ‡

eople enjoy belonging to clubs and organizations. It gives them a sense of belonging, and a shared identity. Knights are no different in this respect. There are a large number of orders that you may be able to join, which will provide you with comradeship and a feeling of importance. Their rituals will help to reinforce your chivalric ideals. You should, however, be wary of who you sign up to.

Religious orders

You are unlikely to want to join a knightly order such as that of the Hospital, whose members are part monk, part knight. Such orders are in clear decline, and you would probably not enjoy the monastic discipline involved.

It was in the early days of the crusades, in the 12th century, that the orders of the Temple and Hospital were founded. They served a valuable purpose when there was a Latin Kingdom in the east, before the loss of its capital, Acre, in 1291. The Order of the Temple was destroyed early in the 14th century. It owned a lot of land in Europe, and had developed into a

54

There are many orders to join, but you cannot become a Templar, as the Order of the Temple is no more. It was destroyed by King Philip IV of France in the early 14th century. Here, some Templar knights are being burned to death for being heretics.

major banking institution. Not surprisingly, Philip IV of France had his eyes on its resources. The Templars were put on trial, with accusations of heresy and vice brought against them; the knights were said to be guilty of blasphemy, of worshipping idols, and of committing an impressive range of sexual misdemeanours. The charges, however, were not always very convincing. They included the following:

> *Item, of the third class, which is about the worship of cats, there are two articles; no witnesses testified about this in England.*

> *He said that after he made the single beds of the Templars, on the next day he would very often find signs of two of them, as if they had slept together.*

Knights of the Order of St James of Santiago. This is a Spanish religious order, which played an important role in the Christian reconquest of Spain. In contrast to the Templars, Hospitallers and Teutonic Knights, these knights are permitted to marry.

The Order of the Hospital subsequently took over much of the property of the Templars. After Acre fell, the order moved its headquarters first to Cyprus and then to Rhodes. If you go on crusade in the Mediterranean, you will undoubtedly have dealings with the Hospitallers, even though they are no longer as significant as they once were. There are other knightly religious orders in the Mediterranean world; you will find in Spain among others the Order of Calatrava and the Order of St James of Santiago.

The Teutonic Knights are another important military order. Their interests have switched from the crusader states in the east to the Baltic, where they have played the major role in organizing crusades against the heathen in Lithuania. The defeat of the Teutonic Knights at Tannenberg (or Grunwald) at the hands of a combined Polish and Lithuanian army in 1410 has put their continued existence in some doubt; it seems unlikely that the order will ever fully recover from this catastrophe.

Secular orders: St George, the Band, and the Garter

Secular orders of knighthood are popular, even though many do not last long. Kings are keen to create them as they add to their prestige and are a useful way of gaining support. The first of the secular orders was the Society of St George, founded in Hungary in 1325; this was closely followed by the Order of the Band, set up in Castile in 1330. A Spanish chronicle recorded this:

> *And they were called the knights of the Band, and they had an ordinance among themselves of many good matters which were all works of chivalry. And when they gave a band to a knight, they made him swear and promise that he would keep to himself all the matters of chivalry that were written in that ordinance.*

Then in 1344 Edward III of England had the idea of creating an Order of the Round Table. This was to have about 300 members, and the king went so far as to begin building a huge round house within Windsor Castle for the meetings of the knights. The chronicler Jean le Bel wrote:

> *He had a general feast and plenary court proclaimed throughout his kingdom, to ordain this Round Table, and he ordered damsels and damoiselles, knights and squires, to come to this great feast at Windsor at Whitsun 1344, without any excuse.*

The intention was to model the new order on the Arthurian past, but for some reason the project was abandoned, even though the round building stood virtually complete. In place of his grand plan, the king created a severely cut-down version four years later, drawing its very selective membership of 26 almost exclusively from those who had fought at Crécy. There were no longer any Arthurian overtones; instead, the order was dedicated to St George, and is known, rather mysteriously, as the Order of the Garter.

Why is it called the Garter, and why are blue and gold its colours?

✝ There is an unlikely suggestion that it is named after the garter that a pretty young lady dropped at a ball, which the king picked up.

✠ It could be that it is called the Garter because the king, as a joke, wanted to call it after some article of underwear, but faced a problem in that there are very few types of underclothes to choose from. You may well speculate what the order might have been called, had a wider selection been available.

Shown here in stained glass is the Garter, with its motto Honi soit qui mal y pense *('Shame on him who thinks ill of it'), which is the symbol of Edward III's order of knighthood.*

✠ A more serious suggestion is that the blue and gold of the Garter was an allusion to Edward III's claim to the French throne, and that the motto, *Honi soit qui mal y pense* ('Shame on him who thinks ill of it') also refers to this.

It is hard to imagine that the Order of the Garter, small, over-exclusive, and with a distinctly odd name and motto, can possibly succeed in the long run. Edward would surely have done better to base his order on a different motto he and his knights used, which went: 'Hey, hey, the White Swan, by God's soul I am thy man.'

Other chivalric orders

There are many other chivalric orders founded by rulers. Not all have been successful. In 1352, King John II of France founded the Company of the Star, with a membership of 300. This was ill-fated. Almost a third of the knights were killed in the battle of Mauron, even before the first annual meeting of the company took place. John's capture at the battle of Poitiers in 1356, and his death in 1364, put paid to the plan.

In the second half of the 14th century the number of orders multiplied considerably. Obviously, orders created by rulers have the greatest prestige, but there are many others that you could join. The duke of Bourbon, for example, has recently set up the order of the *Fer de Prisonnier*, or 'Prisoner's Iron' with a membership of 16 knights, and the count of Foix has created the Enterprise of the Dragon, which women as well as men can join. In Germany there are many tournament societies, the first of which was created in 1361. These associations have an annual meeting, which features jousting, and they are controlled by a council.

A LIST OF ROYAL ORDERS

The Society of St George	Hungary, 1325
The Order of the Band	Castile, 1330
The Order of the Garter	England, 1348
The Order of the Black Swan	Savoy, 1350
The Order of the Star	France, 1352
The Company of the Knot	Naples, 1352
The Order of the Collar	Savoy, 1364
The Golden Shield	France, 1367
The Enterprise of St George	Aragon, 1371
The Order of the Ermine	Brittany, 1381
The Order of the Ship	Naples, 1381
The Order of the Dove	Castile, 1390
The Salamander	Austria, *c.* 1390
The Golden Apple	France, 1395
The Jar of the Salutation	Aragon, 1403

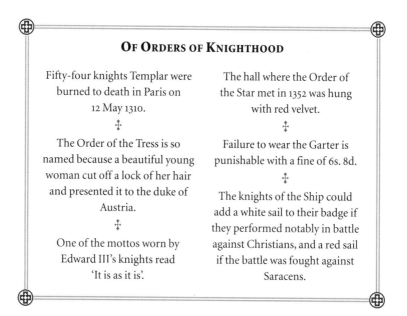

OF ORDERS OF KNIGHTHOOD

Fifty-four knights Templar were burned to death in Paris on 12 May 1310.

✠

The Order of the Tress is so named because a beautiful young woman cut off a lock of her hair and presented it to the duke of Austria.

✠

One of the mottos worn by Edward III's knights read 'It is as it is'.

The hall where the Order of the Star met in 1352 was hung with red velvet.

✠

Failure to wear the Garter is punishable with a fine of 6s. 8d.

✠

The knights of the Ship could add a white sail to their badge if they performed notably in battle against Christians, and a red sail if the battle was fought against Saracens.

Characteristics of an order

The orders vary considerably in detail, but they will all have statutes that set out the mission statement. That for the short-lived Company of the Knot includes the following:

> *Taking up in the name of the same Holy Spirit the Knot itself, which even as it figuratively ties together its parts, connects those who profess it morally in unity, to the sevenfold increase of your strength in faith, and to your strengthening, proceeding from virtue to virtue in work incumbent upon you hereafter.*

The statute will explain the rules of membership, and set out the obligations of the knights towards each other. It will normally give the procedures for the annual general meetings.

The Order of the Ship, founded by Charles III of Naples in 1381, lasted for no more than five years. However, its statutes provide a good example of what you may find when you join an order. The aims of the Ship were laudable:

To give heart and hardiness to all to do well, and to love, honour, and hold dear the good and the valiant, and to hate and despise the bad and the cowardly, as is right, and as the Order wishes and commands.

All members of the order were, among many duties:

✦ To help each other in every way, especially if they fall into poverty, are imprisoned or are ill.

✦ Forbidden to defame any noble woman.

✦ To be fined if they failed to attend the annual general court.

At the court, the knights reported all their adventures, which were then recorded for posterity. Spiritual obligations included fasting every Friday, and saying prayers regularly.

If you became a member of the Ship, you looked good, in a blue jupon, a white surcoat with a silver-gilt hem, red shoes and a red mantle and hood. The idea of the badge of the ship was that you started off with a simple hull and mast; as you distinguished yourself, so you could add elements to it, such as tillers, an anchor, ropes, a yard-arm, sail and banner.

The Company of the Knot was founded in 1352 by King Louis of Naples. The figure in black in the centre, dining alone, is a knight who has disgraced himself.

Many orders have a physical headquarters:

✠ For the Garter, which is linked to a college of clergy, this is in St George's chapel in Windsor Castle, along with various lodgings.

✠ The Star was based at Saint-Ouen; as with the Garter, it was linked to a chapel, with its canons and chaplains.

✠ The Knot had its centre in the Castel dell'Ovo, on an island in the bay of Naples.

✠ The Ship had its meetings in the Castel Nuovo in Naples itself.

Which order to join?

It is difficult to know which order to recommend. Avoid the Garter: it is too small and exclusive. Some new orders look promising, such as the Jar of the Salutation in Aragon. Perhaps the best option is to set up your own. Boucicaut did this, when he created the Order of the White Lady on a Green Shield in 1400. This had thirteen members, and was set up on a trial basis for five years. It was intended to deal with the problem of aristocratic ladies who could not defend themselves or their property against predators. Christine de Pizan, herself a widow, liked the project, and wrote one of her less satisfactory poems about it:

> *Those who, without faltering,*
> *Bear the green shield with a beautiful lady,*
> *Wish, with sharp cutting swords*
> *To protect her against evil-doers.*

Sadly, in the event, Boucicaut's order promised more than it performed, and there are no practical achievements credited to it. You may have better luck.

There is no obligation on you to join an order, but if you do, you will surely find it worthwhile. You should gain prestige from being a member, and it may well be helpful to have the support of the other knights. You will certainly feel all the more chivalric for it.

RECRVITMENT & RETINVES

This indenture is made between the noble men Sir Thomas de Beauchamp, earl of Warwick, on the one hand, and Sir Robert Herle on the other, and it is to be known that Robert will stay with the earl for life, with four men-at-arms for war, to go wherever the earl goes, overseas or at home.

INDENTURE BETWEEN THE EARL OF WARWICK AND ROBERT HERLE, 1339

✣   ✣   ✣

 knight is a member of the elite in any army. You will find that no more than one in four of the cavalry forces are knights, and of course the cavalry are usually greatly outnumbered by the ordinary soldiers who fight on foot.

You will probably hold land in return for performing military service, but by the early 14th century the traditional feudal service, owed for a period of 40 days, had become largely obsolete. In France many nobles and knights were not even sure how much service the king could count on. Many of those who owed service failed to carry it out. In England the quotas of knights that lords were supposed to produce had been radically reduced in the 13th century. The reality is that knights, like other soldiers, expect to be paid, though in times of real emergency voluntary service can be expected. In 1355, for example, when faced with an English invasion, the French nobles offered to serve at their own cost for a month. What you should look for is a fair deal with decent wages and, if you are lucky, lucrative bonuses.

Retinues

As a knight, you will have your own small following or retinue.

- ✝ Hugh Cheyne agreed to serve the earl of March in 1376, and brought with him a chamberlain, three sergeants and a page, with seven horses in all.
- ✝ Jean de Cepoy served Bertrand du Guesclin in 1378 with another knight and 18 squires.

These various small units are combined into larger retinues. The rank above that of knight is banneret; someone of this standing will have a following of perhaps 20 or more. The ideal organization suggested by the French has the cavalry divided into hundreds, each hundred consisting of four bannerets, 16 knights and 80 squires. A royal ordinance of 1374 issued by Charles V specified that the men-at-arms were to be in *routes* of a hundred men, each with a captain. It is very difficult to achieve such regularity in practice, and in reality there is little attempt to standardize the size of retinues; the more important and wealthy a lord is, the larger his following will be. For example:

- ✝ The Black Prince, son of Edward III, had a retinue of 11 bannerets, 102 knights, 264 squires and men-at-arms, and 966 archers in 1346.
- ✝ Bertrand du Guesclin's following in 1378 was composed of 72 companies, in total consisting of 2 bannerets, 90 knights and 567 squires.

In Italy, there was a standard unit, the *barbuta*, which consisted of a knight and his page. By the later 14th century this structure was superseded by the lance, which is formed by three men the knight, squire and page. The first two would fight, with the third looking after the horses and equipment. The lances would be combined into banners, each consisting of about 20 knights.

In addition to the knights, squires, men-at-arms and perhaps archers listed in muster rolls or account books, there are also pages, servants and

RIGHT An Italian knight from the town of Prato in Tuscany, in about 1340. He is fully armed for war, in the latest style of plate armour, with a surcoat worn over it. His horse, a magnificent destrier, or charger, is equipped with a cloth caparison displaying his coat of arms.

BELOW Sir Geoffrey Luttrell being presented with lance, helmet and shield by his wife and daughter-in-law. The image emphasizes his family and his lineage, with the martlets of his coat of arms shown clearly. His horse is barded as befitted a knight, and bears a grand crest. A triangular pennon on the lance is another demonstration of his knightly status.

King Arthur presiding over the Round Table. Legends of Arthur and his Knights of the Round Table are popular – you probably know them already – but you shouldn't take them too seriously.

King Edward III of England in the robes of the Order of the Garter. With only 26 Garter knights, it was a high honour to be among their number. The French created their own order, that of the Star, with 300 knights, soon after the creation of the Garter.

War involves truces, treaties, and formal agreements of all sorts as well as fighting. Here a sealed document is handed over by a group of knights to a king and his followers.

OVERLEAF
Hunting is a popular recreation for the knightly class; it also provides good opportunities to practise using weapons. Gaston Phoebus, the count of Foix, wrote a hunting manual, which he presented to the duke of Burgundy. The page on the left shows knights armed with swords hunting wild boar. The page on the right, also from Gaston Phoebus' hunting manual, shows a group of knights and a lady engaged in falconry; dogs are being used to collect the ducks, herons and other water-birds killed in the sport.

Cy deuise comment on doit ferir le sangler

...t si le sanglé
...n vient cour
...ir sus visai
...ge a visaige
...il doit uenir
...contre luy
...non pas cou
...ant mar tiotant les rnes de
la bride bien courtes. et ne doit
point regarder au sangler ne
a ce quil fera. mar penser en
auiser par ou il pourra mielr
asseoir son coup. et sil fiert de

lespieu il doit ferir de hault en bas
tant comme il pourra ferir en se
leuant sus les estrieux. Et doit
tout uenier cheuauchier court
au corps que long. car il en est
plus apste et moins en grieue
son cheual. car sil monte une
coite il le puet sonstenir sus les
estrieux. et ne grieue une tant
son cheual. et ainsi le puet tour
ner et uirer ca en la et baullier.
et sil cheuauchoit long il ne le
pourroit faire. aussi di ie quil

ABOVE In this tournament scene from a manuscript of Froissart's *Chronicles*, the participants are shown parading through a town. Tournaments are grand events, and the festivities often last for several days. Here heralds display banners with the arms of the king of England as knights on richly caparisoned horses pass below; ladies watch the proceedings.

RIGHT The Jousts at St Inglevert, from a manuscript of Froissart's *Chronicles*. In 1390, three French knights, one of whom was Boucicaut, set up camp at St Inglevert near Calais for a month, and challenged all comers to joust with them. About a hundred Englishmen responded to the challenge; in most cases the French knights triumphed.

ABOVE Court festivities might involve elaborate entertainments. In 1393 there was a disaster when Charles VI of France and five of his friends, dressed as wild men, danced to celebrate of the marriage of one of the queen's ladies in waiting. One of the costumes was set on fire by a torch, and at least four of the dancers died. The king was saved by the duchess of Berry who used her cloak to extinguish his flaming costume.

LEFT It is easy to see how this Swiss knight, Jacob von Warte, was persuaded to take a bath; in this illustration from the *Codex Manesse* he is shown attended by three attractive maidens, while additional water is heated in a cauldron. His helmet and shield are shown hung up on a convenient tree.

RIGHT Walter von Klingen, a follower of the German king Rudolf of Habsburg, is here shown victorious in a joust, unhorsing his opponent. Ladies watch the contest from a balcony above.

other non-combatants. This is demonstrated by details of a contingent sent from Ponthieu to the French army that was defeated at the battle of Courtrai in 1302. The overall total was 5 knights, 20 squires, 1 chaplain, 2 clerks, 6 chamberlains, 61 pages and 1 washerwoman. In all they had 84 horses. So, only about one in four of this total retinue was an active soldier.

These retinues are not solely for war. Many contracts specify service in tournaments as well as war, while a life contract involves attendance on a lord in peacetime.

Choosing a retinue to join

It may be obvious which retinue to join when you go to war. Retinues normally have a core of family members, permanent officials and perhaps tenants, who will campaign regularly with a particular lord. On this basis, your choice may be virtually automatic. However, the composition of a retinue can vary, even from one campaign to the next. If we look at Bertrand du Guesclin's following in 1370–71 we can see that 83 knights served with him at some time during that period. There were ten separate musters held; only one knight was present at all of them, and ten knights at only one. Most served on five or six occasions.

Some lords are much more popular than others. In 1300 a poet praised Robert Clifford in *The Song of Caerlaverock*.

> *I well know there is no degree of praise of which he is not worthy, as he exhibits as many proofs of wisdom and prudence as any of those who accompany his good lord the king... If I were a young maiden, I would give him my heart and person, so great is his fame.*

Men served in Clifford's retinue year after year; that of his contemporary, Henry Percy, on the other hand, showed less continuity in its composition. There are people it might be as well to avoid serving. Marshal Boucicaut may have a great reputation, but would you really want to accompany a man who waters his wine, hears mass twice a day, spends hours in prayer, and insists on reading either pious works or histories of classical heroes? What you should do is to look for someone successful in

PARTNERSHIPS

It is a good idea to enter into an agreement with another knight to be his brother-in-arms. This means that you will look out for each other, providing support and advice. You may well agree to share in the profits and losses inevitable in war; this reduces the financial risks involved in knighthood. Robert Knollys and Hugh Calveley were brothers-in-arms for very many years; these agreements can also be relatively short-lived, like that between Calveley and Bertrand du Guesclin when they fought together in Spain.

A knight holding a standard. Standard-bearers are an obvious target in battle, so it's a dangerous task to take on. You will probably want to ask yourself whether it is worth risking your life for the sake of a banner.

the business of war, with a good record of generosity towards his men. You should also check the wage rates on offer; it is far from unknown for people when subcontracting to pay less to their men than they are receiving for them from the government.

Contracts for service

It is best to make a written agreement when you decide to enter the service of a particular lord. In England, this is done by means of an indenture, a document made in two copies, with each party keeping one. You may make an agreement for a single campaign, or for life. In 1318 Peter de Uvedale contracted by means of an indenture to serve the earl of Hereford for life with four followers in time of peace, and eight for war and tournaments.

> *It is agreed between the noble Humfrey de Bohun, earl of Hereford, on the one side, and Sir Peter de Uvedale, knight, on the other, that is to say that the said Sir Peter will remain with the said earl for life, taking robes and saddles, like his other knight bachelors, and food at court, hay, and oats for four horses, and wages for four lads in time of peace, when he comes to court at the earl's order. And in time of war and for tournaments, hay and oats for eight horses, and wages for eight lads. And compensation for horses of arms lost in war in the earl's service.*

The English are keen to have as much detail as possible of the terms and conditions of service set out in this way. Elsewhere, agreements are normally rather simpler. In France, letters of retainer usually promise pay 'in the customary manner', and are often vague about such matters as the length of service. A French knight agreed to serve the king of Navarre in 1378 in florid language, but without the precision characteristic of English agreements.

> *I promise and swear by these present letters to the excellent and puissant prince, the king of Navarre, my redoubtable lord, that I will serve him and his children well and loyally, in his kingdom and in all of Spain, as long as I am of the said kingdom and Spain, against all and whatsoever persons, of whatever dignity, estate or condition they are and may be, and I will guard his body and his honour from all evil and villainy, and if I know anyone who wishes to commit these, I will prevent them with all my power and will inform the king, my said lord, immediately and without delay, and I will keep and hold his secrets without revealing them in any way, and will continue in his war as long as it lasts.*

The *condotta* was the form of contract used in Italy; the term *condottieri* often used for those who fight there simply means 'contract men'. These contracts were often for relatively short periods of four or six months, but John Hawkwood had four year-long contracts from Florence and one of eight months, in addition to several six-month ones.

If you make a contract with a lord, you have certain expectations:

✝ If the contract is for life, then it is likely that you will be given land, or the income from an estate, as a regular fee.

✝ If you just enter into a contract for a year, then the fee will be a straightforward cash payment.

✝ As a retainer, you will be given robes; it is obviously impressive if you have all of your retinue dressed in the same colours.

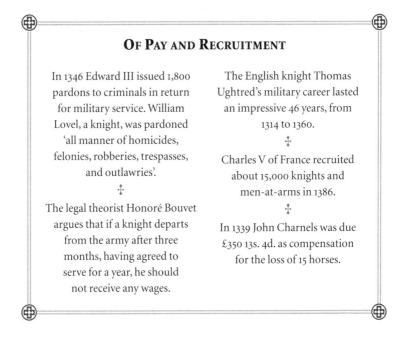

OF PAY AND RECRUITMENT

In 1346 Edward III issued 1,800 pardons to criminals in return for military service. William Lovel, a knight, was pardoned 'all manner of homicides, felonies, robberies, trespasses, and outlawries'.

✝

The legal theorist Honoré Bouvet argues that if a knight departs from the army after three months, having agreed to serve for a year, he should not receive any wages.

The English knight Thomas Ughtred's military career lasted an impressive 46 years, from 1314 to 1360.

✝

Charles V of France recruited about 15,000 knights and men-at-arms in 1386.

✝

In 1339 John Charnels was due £350 13s. 4d. as compensation for the loss of 15 horses.

A clash of mounted knights, fighting with
spear and sword.

✝ Badges may also be provided; in England a particularly notable insignia is the collar of linked S shapes, which is distributed to members of the duke of Lancaster's following.

Pay

The pay you will receive is usually intended not so much as a reward, but more as a subsistence allowance. At the start of the war with France in 1337, however, Edward III offered double wages to those prepared to go overseas to fight, but he could not afford that for long, and soon reverted to the standard two shillings a day for a knight, with half that for a squire.

In France, from the middle of the 14th century wages stabilized at 20 *sous tournois* a day for a knight, with 10 *sous* for a squire.

Money is needed to fight wars. There are many different coins, both silver and gold.
Those below were all minted by the French monarchy.

If you're strapped for cash, you might be better off in Italy where the laws of demand and supply mean that mercenary troops can sometimes negotiate particularly good deals. If you served there with the German mercenary Haneken Bongard in 1358, you would have received 6 florins a month. English soldiers are in higher demand than Germans, and five years later they were receiving 10 florins a month from Florence. In 1384 the authorities in Siena, in a state of panic, recruited lances at the extraordinary rate of 18 florins a month. Hawkwood's salary in 1382 was the highest the city paid to anyone, soldier or official, in the city's service.

In addition to wages, you can hope to receive a bonus. In England, this is known as the regard, and is paid on a quarterly basis. In Italy your bonus may be disguised in the city's accounts as a loan; if mercenaries are in great demand, you may be able to negotiate a good agreement.

Compensation for lost horses

In 1343 Pedro IV of Aragon was faced by angry troops at Barcelona. They demanded their wages, as well as compensation for horses lost on campaign. Pedro told them that he could meet the request for pay, but that he had not agreed to pay for lost horses. There was 'much discussion and many words' about this, and the men were told that they could leave the army if they wished.

Your horse is a major investment, and it is hardly surprising that knights want to have some form of insurance in case it is killed in battle, or dies on campaign. The battle of Crécy resulted in a huge bill for lost horses for the French government to meet. It is not only expensive to provide compensation, but also bureaucratically complex. The horses need to be valued, and checks are needed to prevent fraud. Not surprisingly, in the 1370s the French and English governments gave up making these payments. So, by the late 14th century you would be lucky if you succeeded in negotiating compensation for lost horses.

✠ VII ✠

Ⴕoᴜʀ∩ᴀᴍᴇ∩ᴛ s & Ꭻoᴜꜱᴛs

*It is a recognized rule in this game that he who loses most and is most
frequently unhorsed, is judged the most valiant and the stronger.*

VITA EDWARDI SECUNDI, 1307

✠   ✠   ✠

ournaments and jousts are the great celebrations of chivalry,
and as a knight you will be an enthusiastic participant. These
events will offer you opportunities to demonstrate your skill
in the use of arms. Geoffroi de Charny may explain that the
greatest honour is to be won on the battlefield, but battles are, in fact, quite
rare, and your deeds may well go unnoticed in the chaos and confusion.
You will find it much more satisfactory to prove yourself in tournaments
and jousts. Even if you don't win, you can gain a reputation for courage and
gallantry as you are thrown from your horse.

To be successful on the tournament circuit involves considerable expenditure, as de Charny acknowledges, for you will require good equipment.
You need to be tough, strong and skilful, and if you do well, you will win
great renown. It is impossible to imagine that it will ever be possible to win
such fame in any other sport, such as, say, football (a game for peasants).

Tournaments

Tournaments are not what they used to be. In the 12th century, in many
cases they amounted to arranged battles. There would be a massed charge
at the start, followed by a mêlée. Large numbers, perhaps even up to 3,000,
were involved; knights could be captured and ransomed for profit, horses
could be taken as booty. Fighting was serious, and took place over large

Jousting is a dangerous sport; here a knight, his lance broken, has been thrown from his horse. If this happens to you, remember that it's no bad thing to be a gallant loser.

swathes of countryside. Tournaments still take place with fighting between groups of knights rather than individuals, but the numbers are not as large as in the past, and the contests are normally held within a confined area. There are various ways in which the fighting at a tournament can be organized. You might, for example, find that a wooden castle is constructed, which one group has to defend.

It may seem when you are in the thick of things that there is very little difference between a tournament and a battle, but because there should be no involvement of infantry troops you will not have those dreadful arrows to fear. You are less likely to be killed in a tournament than in battle, and you should not have to pay a ransom if you are on the losing side. Tournaments can be valuable practice for war, even if you use rather different equipment.

There is much formality surrounding tournaments. Before the fighting begins several things must happen:

- ✠ The event needs to be proclaimed and advertised, and judges have to be chosen.
- ✠ The banners, helmets and crests of the participants should be displayed.
- ✠ The two sides who are to fight need to be selected, to make sure that they are equal.

There are festivities, with much dancing and drinking, and a parade of the participants, over the two days before the actual contest begins.

Eventually, on the third day, the fighting takes place. The two sides are held back in roped enclosures; when the word is given, the ropes are cut, and the engagement starts. There will be much shouting as the spectators cheer on their favourites, and trumpets will blare. As the mêlée continues,

Tournaments are not just about fighting. Display and ceremony are important. Here a herald holds the banners of some of the participants.

pages will rush in to pick up the fallen and help them remount. Here Chaucer describes the fighting in a tournament:

There see men who can joust and who can ride,
There shafts are shattered on thick shields,
They feel the blows though the breast-bone.
Up spring the spears, twenty feet high,
Out come the swords, bright as silver,
They hew at the helmets to shatter them.
Out bursts the blood in stern streams red.

Eventually the judges will decide to call time. Trumpets will sound the retreat. In the evening there will be yet more festivities, as the prizes are awarded. They may be for:

✝ The best blow of all (the 'man of the match' award).

✝ Breaking the most lances.

✝ Keeping a helmet on the longest.

There are different forms of mock battle such as the *béhourd*, in which lighter, blunted weapons are used, and relatively flimsy armour, usually made of leather, is worn. These are less serious occasions than tournaments proper, but they give you a good chance to practise your skills.

Jousts

The joust is an individual conflict between two knights; it is distinct and different from the tournament. It will often be agreed that there should be three rounds; the two men ride at each other, aiming to pass each other on the left-hand side, and to strike each other with their lances. This began to be popular in the 13th century; jousting frequently takes place before the tournament proper begins, often on the previous day.

A particularly famous jouster of the past was the German knight Ulrich von Liechtenstein, who wrote up his experiences in verse. Ulrich, rather unusually, enjoyed cross-dressing, and described a journey he made dressed as the goddess Venus, during which he took part in innumerable jousts and tournaments, all for the unrequited love of his lady.

> *Thus like a woman I was dressed*
> *And all I had was of the best.*
> *The peacock feathers on my hat*
> *Were rather dear, I'll tell you that.*

Ulrich was eccentric in other ways. On one occasion he even ordered a bath, during which two pages poured rose petals all over him, an experience which, curiously, he seems to have enjoyed. If you are considering

Jousting knights, from an English manuscript. Their shields and helmets are in the latest fashion, and their horses are fully caparisoned, displaying their coats of arms.

Scoring

Scoring systems are complex, and will vary from event to event. In jousting, the top score normally comes for unhorsing your opponent; breaking your lance is the next best action; striking your opponent on the helmet comes third. The tournament's overall prize, the 'man of the match' award, will be given to the knight who has most distinguished himself, and there may well be differing views on that. It could be that someone who has been unhorsed several times has shown conspicuous bravery, and deserves to be well rewarded.

taking part in tournamets under a pseudonym, then that of Ulrich would be a good one to choose, but it might be better to claim to come from Gelderland rather than his real homeland of Styria.

There is a lot of technique to learn if you want to be a skilled jouster. Controlling your horse properly is important, but it is not easy with so many things to think about at the same time. You have to make sure that your horse takes a straight line, and does not veer off course, or even worse, cross in front of the other jouster. In Spain they have taken to erecting a barrier between the two jousters, so as to avert this, but no one has yet thought of introducing it in France or England.

Do not be tempted to impress by using an oversized lance: if you strike a low blow with a heavy lance, and your opponent strikes you a high blow with a lighter lance, he will unseat you. A medium-sized manageable lance will be much better than a great big one that will unbalance you and pull you out of your saddle. Your horse will go much better if you have a lighter

OPPOSITE *The knight on the left will have a good score from this bout. He's unhorsed his opponent and broken his lance. The barrier, or list, shown here dividing the combatants was developed in Spain a few years ago.*

lance. Think about what your opponent is doing, and adjust your own tactics accordingly. It is tempting to close your eyes just before the moment of impact. Don't do this. Be careful not to turn your shoulder away; Edward Beauchamp made this mistake in a joust in 1381, and was knocked off his horse as a result.

Ulrich von Liechtenstein was expert in jousting techniques. He wrote a boastful account of one of his bouts:

> I turned a little from the man
> (to knock him sprawling was my plan)
> I struck him in the collar then.
> I turned and jousted with such skill
> Sir Otte almost took a spill.

Here are a few key points to remember:

- ✠ Ride upright, with long stirrups, holding the reins in your left hand.
- ✠ Use a lance of manageable weight.
- ✠ Make sure your helmet is on straight, and that you have a good line of sight.
- ✠ Hold your lance in the palm of your hand, not just with your fingers.
- ✠ Do not let the tip of your lance tilt up or down.
- ✠ Do not twist, or turn your shoulder.
- ✠ If your opponent always aims for the same place, vary your own tactics.
- ✠ Keep your eyes fixed on the target, not on the tip of your lance.

The jousts of St Inglevert

A good example of jousting is the notable set of encounters that took place outside Calais, then as now in English hands, over a month in 1390. Do not get involved in something of this sort unless you are really expert.

Three Frenchmen, Boucicaut, Renaud de Roye and the lord of Sempy, set up camp at St Inglevert, and announced that they were ready to combat anyone who accepted their challenge. Two shields were set up, one to symbolize jousts of war, and the other jousts of peace (which would take place with blunted weapons). Challengers had to ride up and strike one of the shields. This was during a period of truce; the occasion was part sporting event, part incident of war. About a hundred English challengers appeared, all selecting to fight jousts of war. There were doubts that the three Frenchmen were strong enough; it would need great stamina to fight so often. In the event, both Boucicaut and Roye were so badly bruised in the course of the jousts that they had to rest for over a week.

A particularly dramatic encounter was that between John Clifton and Renaud de Roye:

- ✝ Round One. Each man struck the other on the helmet.
- ✝ Round Two. Each man hit the other's shield; both dropped their lances.
- ✝ Round Three. Each man hit the other high on the helmet, striking sparks.
- ✝ Round Four. The horses failed to go straight.
- ✝ Round Five. Both men broke their lances.
- ✝ Round Six. Each man hit the other on the helmet; both helmets came off.

OPPOSITE *A jousting helmet and shield.*

RIGHT *A French banner.*

There was no provision for a tie-break; honour was equal, and the two knights were greatly praised for their achievements.

The jousting at St Inglevert was accompanied by grand dinners and much festivity; this was a great social occasion, as well as a supreme test of skill and endurance.

Combat with a range of weapons

By the end of the last century, challenges to fight were being issued involving not just jousting on horseback, but a range of military activities, notably fighting with swords, axes and daggers. Nowadays, a combat often takes the form of four rounds, each using a different weapon. In 1377 a tournament took place on three sites, St Omer, Ardres and Calais, between 12 knights from England and Hainault, and 14 from France. There were to be separate rounds on horseback, and on foot with lance, sword and dagger. You may be tempted to take part in an event that offers a supreme

LEFT *Make sure you go to a tournament well prepared – you may have to fight with daggers as well as your sword and lance.*

BELOW *Nowadays it is increasingly common for knights to challenge each other to fight on foot, reflecting the reality of warfare. A range of weapons can be used; the illustration shows knights fighting with poleaxes.*

test of your skills in the use of weapons, but be careful. This sort of fighting can be dangerous, and perhaps because of this, challenges often end in lengthy arguments rather than actual combat.

In 1400 an Aragonese squire, Michael d'Orris, issued a challenge to the knights of England. He had vowed to wear an uncomfortable piece of leg armour until he had fought an English knight. He set out the terms of the fight in detail.

Ten strokes with the battle-axe, without intermission, and when these strokes have been given, and the judge shall cry out 'Ho!', ten cuts with the sword to be given without intermission or change of armour. When the judge shall cry out 'Ho!', we will resort to our daggers and give ten stabs with them. Should either party lose or drop his weapon, the other may continue until the judge shall cry out 'Ho!'.

After the fight on foot, the two opponents were to joust until one fell, or was so wounded he could continue no further. John Prendergast accepted the challenge, but, there being no postal service, letters were delayed, and arguments ensued. Insults began to be traded. 'I hold your conduct as very discourteous and ungentlemanly', wrote d'Orris. Prendergast finally demanded £333 expenses from the Aragonese, and, some four years after the initial challenge was made, the matter was dropped. No fight ever took place. It is better not to get into such arguments to begin with.

Spectacle and propaganda

Tournaments are sometimes disapproved of by governments and the Papacy; they can be seen as a dangerous distraction. That is the English king Henry V's view today. Even Edward I, a keen participant in tournaments in his youth, prohibited them when he considered that they were drawing knights away from his war against the Scots. It was impossible, however, to prevent such popular events from taking place, and in 1316 the Papacy gave up trying and withdrew its objections. In 1338 Philip IV of France banned tournaments during the war with the English, but Edward III, in contrast, gave them his full encouragement. He considered them a way of encouraging knights and nobles to join in his royal enterprises. Alfonso XI of Castile was another enthusiast for tournaments, regarding them as useful practice for war; one was to take place at every meeting of his knightly order of the Band.

There is a strong dramatic element to many tournaments:

- ✠ In 1331 a tournament was held in Cheapside in London which began with a procession in which maidens led knights dressed as Tatars through the streets.

- ✠ In 1359 Edward III and his sons, together with a group of nobles, dressed up as the mayor and aldermen of London for a tournament.

- ✠ In 1362 a Cheapside tournament saw seven knights dressed as the Seven Deadly Sins jousting against all comers.

The fashion for staging tournaments with historical or mythological themes probably started in the Low Countries, where they developed as civic festivals. If you attend an event billed as a 'Round Table', however, you will probably find that scenes echoing the Arthurian past are played out. At these in particular, drinking and dancing are much more important than fighting. Increasingly, the show and the spectacle seems to be taking over from the sport, and you may find that you are spending more on fancy dress than on proper equipment.

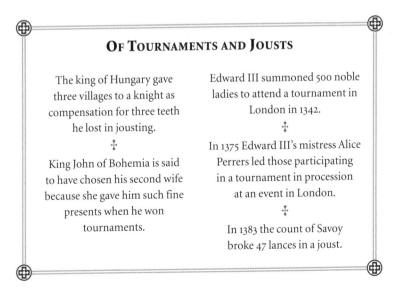

Tournaments are used to celebrate great royal occasions. The entry of Queen Isabeau to Paris in 1389 was marked by much pageantry, and by a tournament involving 60 knights. Unfortunately the horses' hooves kicked up so much dust that it was hard to see what was happening, even when the ground was watered for the second

OF TOURNAMENTS AND JOUSTS

The king of Hungary gave three villages to a knight as compensation for three teeth he lost in jousting.

✝

King John of Bohemia is said to have chosen his second wife because she gave him such fine presents when he won tournaments.

Edward III summoned 500 noble ladies to attend a tournament in London in 1342.

✝

In 1375 Edward III's mistress Alice Perrers led those participating in a tournament in procession at an event in London.

✝

In 1383 the count of Savoy broke 47 lances in a joust.

RIGHT *It is important to look your best at a tournament – this is a prime opportunity to impress damsels.*

OPPOSITE *If you want to show off, you can wear an elaborate crest on your helmet. These are for jousts and tournaments, not for war.*

day's events. The conclusion, however, was more satisfactory, for it took place indoors, in a great hall built for the purpose. There Boucicaut and other knights entertained the ladies by jousting for two hours.

Prizes

You should not expect to win much in a tournament, save glory and, if you are really fortunate, the hand of a fair maiden. You might get a title. Giles of Argentein became the knight of the Greenwood as a result of one of his many tournament successes; he was later rated the third-best knight in all of Christendom. Examples of prizes include:

- ✠ London, 1390. A horn with gold mounts; a greyhound with a gold collar; a gold circlet; a gold belt.

- ✠ Florence, 1406. A silver-gilt lion and a velvet cap; a helmet with a silver dragon's head; a jousting helm with two wings decorated with coloured feathers.

You can also win horses, though not as the main prizes. If you manage to strike your opponent so that he comes completely off his horse, the animal is yours. Equally, if you are struck with a foul blow, you can claim your opponent's horse. What happens if both you and your opponent come off is a moot point and so open to debate; this was a problem set by Geoffroi de Charny, but his answer is not recorded.

Be careful

Even though many tournaments are dominated more by the ceremonies than the fighting, you still need to take care. Lances are dangerous, and tragedies can occur. Take heed of these cautionary events:

- ✠ John Mortimer was killed in a tournament in 1318.
- ✠ In 1344 Raoul, count of Eu and constable of France, died after being struck by a lance in the jousts held to celebrate Philip VI's marriage.
- ✠ William Montague, earl of Salisbury, killed his own son in a tournament in 1382.

It is not just lances you must watch out for, however – there are dangers in the festivities that accompany tournaments too. Even fancy dress can be hazardous. In 1393 the king of France and several of his courtiers dressed up as wild men. One of them was accidentally set on fire by a torch, and several perished in the conflagration. Health and safety is not what it should be in the French court.

✠ VIII ✠

CAMPAIGNING

*When we are in the fields, on our swift war-horses, our shields
at our necks and our lances lowered, and the great cold
numbs us all, our limbs fail us both before and behind, and
our enemies are approaching us.*

THE VOWS OF THE HERON, MID-14TH CENTURY

✠   ✠   ✠

uch of the time campaigning is no fun; it is a hard, relentless slog. You will hope that there will be great deeds of chivalry to perform, but all too often you will be riding through a desolate countryside, failing to make contact with your enemy.

When to campaign

You need to be ready to campaign at any time of the year, and you probably won't have much choice in the matter. It is obviously best to go when the weather is good and food is plentiful. That means late summer. You will note that the English fought the battle of Crécy on 26 August and Poitiers on 19 September. It is, however, not always possible to arrange matters so conveniently, and you may find yourself in the field later in the year.

✠ Autumn campaigning, particularly in northern Europe, normally means mud, as fields are churned up by men, horses and carts.

✠ Winter brings snow; you will be bitterly cold on expeditions in the Baltic lands in winter. Snow was more unexpected in Lombardy in February 1339 when the battle of Parabiago was fought.

✝ Spring brings better weather for campaigning, but food is in short supply. In northern Italy the melting snows of the Alps mean swollen rivers in Lombardy, making things difficult for armies on the move.

✝ Summer is the best time for campaigning, but it can be very hot, particularly in southern Europe.

You can, and perhaps should, decide when to campaign by using scientific methods. When John Hawkwood's men marched out of Padua at half past five in the morning on 11 January 1391, this precise timing was on the advice of his astrologer Alessio Nicolai.

Muster

There is a lot of work to be done when an army musters. Lists have to be drawn up of the men in their various contingents, and in some cases agreements over pay may have to be finalized. There will probably be discussions over who is to serve in which of the main battalions in the army, and how they are to be drawn up for battle.

A muster is likely to take several days, as the troops gradually arrive. The waiting can be tedious, and you are unlikely to find that there is any training provided to keep you occupied.

Camp

If you read Vegetius on the art of war, you will discover how well organized the Romans were with their camps, which were all carefully planned and laid out. You will not find anything like that happening today. As the army marches, harbingers will be sent out in advance to find suitable lodgings. With luck, there may be a town or village in which houses can be commandeered for the army's use. The marshal has the job of determining who should go where, but all too often it is a matter of every man for himself. There is no question of tents being available for everyone. Chaucer described Sir Topaz:

ABOVE *Commanders get elaborate tents, while ordinary soldiers make do with primitive shelters, as this detail from a fresco in Siena shows.*

LEFT *If an enemy breaks into a camp, tents offer no protection, and are easy to collapse.*

And because he was a knight adventurous,
He would not sleep in any house,
But lay down in his hood;
His bright helmet was his pillow,
And by him his charger grazed
On herbage fine and good.

95

On the English campaign against the Scots in 1327, knights as well as ordinary soldiers had to sleep in the open, close to the river Tyne, holding their horses' reins. It can be different if you are part of a very large slow-moving army, for then it should be possible to make use of the tents and other equipment that is kept in the baggage train. There is a description of the camp on the English expedition to Scotland in 1300 in *The Song of Caerlaverock*:

> *We were quartered by the Marshal, and then might be seen houses built without carpenters or masons, of many different fashions, and many a cord stretched, with white and coloured cloth, with many pins driven into the ground, many a large tree cut down to make huts; and leaves, herbs, and flowers gathered in the woods, which were strewed within; and then our people took up their quarters.*

Accounts show that the king, Edward I, had a great leather tent, and 20 new canvas ones for the campaign; it all sounds very attractive. Yet the reality can be pretty uncomfortable. You are unlikely to find any proper latrine arrangements. If it rains, even the grandest tent will spring a leak.

On the march

The procedure for preparing to march is normally as follows:

- ✝ Banners are carried out and set up, so that everyone knows where to go.
- ✝ At the first blast of the trumpets, the horses must be rounded up, given oats and saddled.
- ✝ At the second blast of the trumpets, you should eat.
- ✝ At the third, put your armour on and take up your weapons.
- ✝ At the fourth, mount your horse and go to the correct banner. Then, move off.

A full-scale army on the march is a magnificent sight. The scene when Edward I set out into southwestern Scotland in 1300 was described at the time, again in *The Song of Caerlaverock*:

> *On the appointed day the whole host was ready, and the good King with his household, then set forward against the Scots, not in coats and surcoats, but on powerful and costly chargers; and that they might not be taken by surprise, well and securely armed. There were many rich caparisons embroidered on silks and satins; many a beautiful pennon fixed to a lance; and many a banner displayed. And afar off was the noise heard of the neighing horses: mountains and valleys were everywhere covered with sumpter horses and wagons with provisions, and sacks of tents and pavilions.*

You will probably find that the army is not very well organized, and that you are not all made to march in a set order. There should, however, be a vanguard, a main body and a rearguard. Scouts should be sent ahead to spy out the land. In practice, the various columns may well take different routes, and there will be lots of stragglers. The cavalry will probably get well ahead of the infantry in the course of the day, and the baggage train may get left far behind. The whole army will be spread out over a wide expanse of countryside. A huge host, complete with large numbers of infantry and encumbered with a baggage train, moves slowly. It took Edward III's army a month to go from Calais to Reims in 1359, an average of about 5 or 6 miles a day.

An army on the march. A column of troops can stretch for many miles.

A mounted raid, or *chevauchée*, is a different matter. The Black Prince, on his 1355 raid from Gascony to Narbonne, could manage 25 miles a day and more. You will be exhausted by a fast ride, as King Pedro IV of Aragon discovered in 1364:

> *When we dismounted, we complained of the long day we had passed, for we had not dismounted during the whole day, eating in our saddles, we and all our people. And when we had dismounted we threw ourselves on a bed, complaining of the toil our person had suffered and that a few of such forced marches would suffice.*

Such campaigning is tough on horses as well as on men. On the Black Prince's raid in 1355 there was no water for them, so in desperation they were given wine to drink. The next day saw them staggering around, unable to keep a secure footing; many were lost as a result.

Food

Don't expect a campaign to be a gastronomic tour. What you are likely to experience is, according to the Spaniard Gutierre Diaz de Gamez, 'mouldy bread or biscuit, meat cooked or uncooked; today enough to eat and tomorrow nothing, little or no wine.' You will, however, need to eat a lot; campaigning is hard work. The basic food is bread, made of coarsely ground grain. You will probably get some kind of pottage, again made from grain, stewed with dried beans and peas. What there is by way of meat and fish will largely depend on what can be captured; armies live off the land when they can. The Scots have a good way of dealing with cattle they take – they skin them, and then boil up the meat in a bag made from the animal's hide. When Pedro IV of Aragon invaded Majorca in 1343, his infantry, the almogàvers, 'overran the land and brought in many animals, large and small, so that our host had enough meat'.

Obviously, you should never drink the water. You won't be used to it, and if you do drink it, you will almost certainly be very ill the next day. An important part of the job of providing provisions for the army is to ensure that there is enough wine and ale. It is a disaster if this goes wrong; when the English army in Scotland in 1356 had nothing but rainwater to drink, the campaign had to be abandoned. The quantities of drink needed are very considerable, for you can reckon on a man needing about a gallon a day. Getting drunk is one way of dealing with the miseries of campaigning.

When on campaign, you can face big problems if the enemy are wise to what is happening, and empty the land in advance of your invasion. This makes it very difficult for an army; it is said that when the English invaded Scotland in 1322 all they found was one lame cow.

The supply of food is vital for the success of any campaign. Here, in a scene from the Luttrell Psalter, *a grand banquet is being prepared, such as might be held to celebrate a victory.*

Even when food is plentiful, you are told by de Charny that a knight ought to be frugal. Marshal Boucicaut insisted on the following:

- ✝ Only one kind of meat.
- ✝ No exotic or unusual sauces.
- ✝ Wine to be diluted with water.
- ✝ Dishes to be of tin or wood, not gold or silver.

That is one ideal; you may well feel that you deserve a proper treat if, say, your army captures a town and you find that there is a lot of food available. You can take spices with you to improve the diet; Henry Bolingbroke's baggage when he went on crusade included ginger, cloves, sugar candy, nutmeg, pepper, saffron and caraway seeds. It is not a good idea, however, to be too fussy about food; don't be like Gaston, count of Foix, who would only eat the wings and thighs of poultry.

The diet on campaign is not good for your teeth. The bread contains a great deal of grit from being milled by hand on portable millstones, and as you chew it, it will grind down your back teeth until they are flat.

Ravaging the land

One of the main weapons available to an army is the destruction of enemy territory. The *chevauchée* is capable of doing immense damage. John Wingfield described the Black Prince's raid of 1355 in a letter:

> *And, my lord, you will be glad to know that my lord has raided the county of Armagnac and taken several walled towns there, burning and destroying them, except for certain towns which he garrisoned. Then he went into the viscounty of Rivière, and took a good town called Plaisance, the chief town of the area, and burnt it and laid waste the surrounding countryside.*

The letter continues with a long list of places burned and destroyed. One chronicle reported that 11 fine cities and 3,700 villages had been devastated in the course of the Black Prince's raid. Fire is the key weapon. As Henry V has it, 'War without fire is like sausages without mustard.' For Pedro IV of Aragon it was a normal part of war, and he described the progress of his army on one campaign in a very matter-of-fact way:

> *We slept first at Murviedo, then at Alcubles, burning and ravaging the land of the said Don Pedro as we went. And we found it abandoned and burnt everything.*

You will probably find that you can leave the actual work of destruction to the common soldiers. The mercenary companies in Italy even employ specialist devastators, called *guastatori*. In 1371 the mercenaries Lutz von

Landau and Federigo of Brescia conducted a savage raid, which saw some 2,000 houses burnt down. There was nothing left standing in the town of Mugnano di Creta after they set fire to it. Wooden houses are easy to set alight, and even stone ones will have inflammable wooden floors and perhaps thatched roofs.

Livestock can be killed, or better, stolen. John Hawkwood is said to have taken over 1,200 oxen and over 15,000 pigs and sheep in a single raid in Italy in 1385. If you take cattle and sheep from the estates of a wealthy monastery, it will probably want to buy them back, and you can then go in and drive them off again.

It is not a good idea to kill all the inhabitants; much better to ransom them. Even peasants can be made to pay for their freedom. On one occasion Haneken Bongard got 31 florins as ransom for each peasant he took from the estates of a wealthy hospital. The chronicler Jean de Venette was one of the few who was sympathetic to the French peasantry:

> *The only desire of the nobles was to ruin the peasants and to work them to death and to give them no protection against their adversaries. Thus the wretched peasants were oppressed on all sides, by friend and foe alike, and could cultivate their vineyards and field only by paying tribute to both sides.*

Knights and men-at-arms attacking a group of peasants. The laws and conventions of war provide little real protection for unarmed civilians, and peasants often suffer greatly at the hands of soldiers.

You may think that this behaviour runs contrary to some of those chivalric concepts that you accepted when you became a knight. In *The Tree of Battles*, by the theorist Honoré Bouvet, the author puts forward an argument that the poor should not suffer:

> *If I wanted to decide that there was honour or valour in attacking a poor innocent who has nothing more in mind than to eat his dry bread alongside his sheep in the fields, or under a hedge or thicket, by my soul, I could not do it.*

Bouvet complained that warfare directed against the labouring people was contrary to the traditions of chivalry, and that warriors should be concerned to maintain justice and protect widows, orphans and the poor. In practice, you probably will not be very bothered about this. Pillage and plunder are necessary in war, and it is the rank and file who carry out the unpleasant part of the work, not the knights. Burning territory does not involve killing people unless they are foolish enough to try to stop you. In any case, peasants are no part of the chivalric world, and if they had you at their mercy, they would show no kindness, so why be kind to them? In the peasant rising in France in 1358 the peasants roasted a knight and forcibly fed bits of him to his own wife and children.

Discipline

According to *The Tree of Battles*, death should be the penalty for a range of offences. The list includes:

- ✝ Striking your commander.
- ✝ Revealing secrets to the enemy.
- ✝ Killing your companion-in-arms.
- ✝ Killing yourself.

It is a little difficult to see how the penalty could be applied in the last case. All this makes discipline sound very severe, but in practice it is not maintained with such rigour. It is particularly hard to impose if the men are not paid wages. As a knight, you will expect to be imposing discipline, rather than being on the receiving end of it.

Discipline in an army is the responsibility of the marshals and constables, and you could find yourself acting as their deputy. Much of what they have to do is prevent men stealing from each other and committing similar minor crimes. You have to be careful on the march to make sure that no one goes in front of the banners that lead the host; to do so is a serious offence. Shouting out orders such as 'To horse!' when you are not entitled to do so is also a major transgression. You need to keep control of the men under your command; a French ordinance of 1374 makes you responsible for all their actions.

The English have produced some elaborate military regulations. Richard II issued a set in 1385, and Henry V, a notably stern disciplinarian, has gone right over the top, producing four military ordinances. These are very detailed. They cover the obvious problems such as ensuring that men keep watch properly, and making sure that no one rides off without orders. You have to obey the instructions of the harbingers about billeting. Regulations set out the procedures to be followed when prisoners are taken; you cannot ransom them without the permission of your captain. Henry's orders even go so far as preventing you from telling jokes about an Englishman, an Irishman and a Welshman.

Boucicaut, as marshal of France, was much concerned with matters of discipline, but his *Life* gives few details of how he actually exercised his role. He did, however, take care to appoint experienced officers under him; anyone who disobeyed them would be punished. Prig that he was, he forbad gambling with dice, and threatened anyone who swore with severe punishment. You may well doubt, however, if in practice it is possible to stop soldiers swearing.

In 1370 Robert Knollys faced a major discipline problem, which he could not resolve. He had led a large raid into France, the first time an operation of such size had been launched without an earl in command. It did not go well, for the French were learning how to deal with this kind of operation, by harassing it and emptying the land. Discipline collapsed, as John Minsterworth and others mutinied. They objected to Knollys as a

SIR ROBERT KNOLLYS

A Cheshire man, Knollys first appeared fighting in Brittany in the 1340s. In 1356 he campaigned with the duke of Lancaster in Normandy. He conducted notable damaging raids in central France in 1358–59, and fought in Brittany and Spain in the 1360s. Despite the failure of his raid in France in 1370, Knollys continued to take a leading part in the war, and in 1382 was influential in putting down the Peasants' Revolt in England. He was a brother-in-arms of Hugh Calveley, another Cheshire man, and war brought him considerable wealth. He died in 1407.

commander on the grounds that he was their social inferior. Such incidents are rare; normally, military expertise such as Knollys possessed is properly respected.

It is not always easy to maintain discipline in a mercenary company. John Hawkwood had to threaten William Gold and his companions with execution when his orders were disobeyed. There is a story of how Hawkwood dealt with two of his men who were quarrelling over a pretty young nun by stabbing her, so denying her to either of them. This tale, however, is probably propaganda put out by the great commander's enemies.

Medical care

You want to do your best to ensure that you do not require medical attention on campaign; if you do need it, it will probably be unpleasant. Take the example of Bertrand du Guesclin, who was knocked out by stones, and then thrown into the moat at the siege of Melun. So as to revive him, the French buried him up to his neck in a dung heap; the warmth of the manure duly did the trick.

If you need a surgeon, you would do well to find someone like Henri de Mondeville, who served Philip IV of France. He had military experience, taught at Montpellier and wrote a vast textbook on surgery and medicine. If you need sensible advice on how, for example, to amputate a gangrenous limb, it is all there in his book. It explains that the way to remove a crossbow bolt from a man's knee is to get someone to hit its point with a hammer, while protecting the joint itself from the blow.

The noted English surgeon John of Arderne had soldiers among his patients. He was a proctologist, and wrote a book on the subject, called *De Fistula in Ano*, about a rather unpleasant condition that may be caused by spending long hours in the saddle. The main treatment he recommends, apart from surgery, is the use of enemas; he is also likely to suggest a hot bath. You will almost certainly want to avoid such advice.

Surgeons can on occasion do a good job. At the battle of Shrewsbury in 1403 the prince of Wales was wounded by an arrow, which struck close to the left side of his nose, leaving the barb deeply embedded. Initial attempts to deal with this by giving the prince drinks of various concoctions failed; then the surgeon John Bradmore made a special instrument, like a pair of tongs, which he used to extract the arrowhead. Your problem, if you are

Surgery is to be avoided if at all possible. This illustration from a treatise on surgery by Roger of Salerno shows a doctor examining various wounds; it seems unlikely that he was able to cure any of these patients.

wounded, may be that surgeons are few and far between. They may even be reluctant to act. The Spanish knight Pero Niño had to take over on one occasion, when a surgeon was too frightened to cauterize a massive wound on a ship's captain's leg, and did the job himself with a white-hot iron.

Never mind battle, however – the great killer in this period is plague, which arrived in the west in 1347; a Genoese ship brought it from the siege of Caffa in the Crimea. In the first serious outbreak it killed about half of the population, but in some places the death rate was much higher than that. Curiously, however, it has not disrupted campaigning as much as you might expect. It meant that there were no major expeditions mounted in the years immediately after plague first struck, but there are no examples of campaigns being abandoned as a result of an army suffering from an outbreak. There is, in any case, nothing that you can do about plague. No one is clear as to its causes, and doctors have no methods of curing it.

OF CAMPAIGNING

You will probably get sunburned on campaign, and if you want to keep your tan, the French doctor Henri de Mondeville suggests you use a mixture of egg white and wheat flour on your face.

✜

Edward III's army of 1359 took leather coracles in the baggage train, so as to ensure a supply of fish.

✜

On the 1382 campaign in Flanders, the French, after a false alarm, spent the night standing knee-deep in mud.

According to Geoffroi de Charny, you should not try to be knowledgeable about good dishes and fine sauces, and should not spend any time deciding which wine to drink.

✜

If you tie a loaf of bread to your saddle, it will taste of horse's sweat when you get to eat it.

✜

When the king of France, Charles VI, went mad for the first time, he unsheathed his sword and chased everyone in sight. This brought the campaign he was on to an end.

Feats of arms

You may well feel that you are not doing as much fighting as you would like on campaign, and that you do not have enough opportunities to display your skills. While ravaging the countryside may give you some pleasure, you will naturally want to have the chance to show off, to ride your charger and wield your lance. The answer for a knight is to issue challenges, and to persuade opponents to come and fight on equal terms. These jousts of war are closer to the tournament in character than to battle proper.

There is a tradition of single combat taking place before battle. In 1333 a gigantic Scotsman called Turnbull challenged an English knight, Robert Benhale, before the battle of Halidon Hill, and was roundly defeated. Since then, such fights between enemies have become much more common, and will provide you with excellent opportunities to display your jousting skills. A typical encounter was that between a French knight and the Englishman Robert Colville during the 1346 campaign. The Frenchman issued a challenge to single combat 'for the love of his lady'. He and Colville had two rounds of jousting, but abandoned the third, as the French knight's shield was broken.

In 1382 a young French knight, Tristan de Roye, learning that peace had been concluded between Castile and Portugal, sent a herald to the English under the earl of Cambridge, asking that someone should engage him in single combat. An English squire, Miles Windsor, anxious to be knighted, accepted. A large number of English knights accompanied him to Badajos where the fight was to take place. He was duly knighted before the engagement. Each man had three lances; each time they were shattered. Shields and armour were battered and split, but neither man was injured. Everyone thought that this was splendid, for honour was duly satisfied on both sides.

In such jousts, rules are applied. On one occasion, in 1379, an English knight, William Farrington, slipped, piercing his opponent through the thigh as he fell. This was disgraceful, and the earl of Buckingham was furious. William apologized fulsomely for his mistake, and was pardoned for the foul blow. In these fights, the issues between England and France are not so important. What is primarily at stake is personal honour.

Engaging in such feats of arms will enhance your prestige, but before you issue any challenges, think carefully about the dangers.

CRUSADE

He has journeyed to Lithuania, and to Russia,
No Christian man of his rank has been so often.
He has also been in Granada, at the siege
Of Algeciras, and he has ridden in Almeria.
He was at Ayas, and at Satalia,
When they were taken, and in the Mediterranean
He has been in many a noble army.

CHAUCER, THE PROLOGUE TO *THE CANTERBURY TALES*,
LATE 14TH CENTURY

✠   ✠   ✠

 oing on crusade should be the high point of a knightly career. The traditional crusading goal was to travel to Jerusalem, so as to recapture it from the Muslims for Christianity, but times have changed. You can go on crusade in many places. Remember Chaucer's knight, who did not fight in France, but went crusading in Alexandria, in Prussia and Latvia, and in Spain. He fought on the shores of the Mediterranean and the Baltic. His was a noble record. If you are keen on travel, crusading offers some splendid opportunities. More than that, crusading enables you to fight in the service of the church. It combines the religious idealism of knighthood with the practical realities of fighting. If with a slash of your sword you kill an infidel, you will have done a great deed in God's eyes. Should you be unfortunate enough to be killed by a finely tempered Damascus sword blade in the hands of a Mamluk or Turkish warrior, you have a first-class ticket to heaven. Salvation beckons to the crusader.

Problems

There are considerable difficulties in this period for crusaders, and you need to think hard before taking part in a holy war. Acre, the last city held by the crusaders in the Holy Land, fell to Muslim forces in 1291, and nowadays it is simply not possible to repeat the feats of previous centuries. There are no longer crusader states to be defended. Above all, there is no hope of regaining Jerusalem, the golden city that lies at the centre of the world. If you want to go there, it has to be as a pilgrim not as a crusader.

Christendom is on the back foot. The Mamluks in Egypt and Syria have powerful armies, but an even bigger danger comes from the Ottoman Turks. Their rise began about a hundred years ago. Bursa in Asia Minor was established as their capital in 1326, and then the Ottomans advanced into the Balkans. By 1385 Sofia was in their hands. In 1389 under Sultan Murad I they won a great victory at Kosovo, where the Balkan princes were defeated. There are new threats from the peoples of central Asia; Timur, or Tamurlane, who died in 1405, was a great leader who built a huge empire.

Before you go on crusade, you should take note of the sad case of Giles of Argentein. He was a knight of great renown, considered by some to have

Chaucer's knight, in The Canterbury Tales, *was a great crusader. Chaucer probably based his career on the life of Philippe de Mézières, a propagandist for the crusade.*

been the third-best knight in all Christendom. He went to the Mediterranean in 1311 to crusade, and was captured not by Muslims, but by Greek Christians based at Rhodes. He was imprisoned at Salonica, and it took a major diplomatic effort by the English to secure his release in 1313.

The Mediterranean and the Balkans

If you are still insistent on taking the cross, there are possibilities for expeditions in the Mediterranean, even though there is little hope of bringing the western kingdoms together for a big expedition in the style of the great crusades of the past. There have been plans for launching a large-scale crusade, and treatises have been written, notably by a French lawyer, Pierre Dubois, and a Venetian, Marino Sanudo, about how this can be done. The theories have proved very hard to put into practice.

✠ There were hopes in the 1330s that the kings of France and England might join together on a crusade, but instead they ended up fighting each other.

✝ King Peter I of Cyprus went on a tour of Europe to recruit crusaders, and to take part in a great many tournaments. He organized an expedition in 1365 that, astonishingly, succeeded in capturing Alexandria in Egypt, though it was soon lost again. The crusaders did, however, acquire a good deal of booty.

In the absence of large expeditions, you can always join in small-scale attacks on Mediterranean ports, but these are unlikely to achieve much, as Geoffroi de Charny found when he joined an expedition that attacked Izmir. In 1390 the duke of Bourbon's attack on the Tunisian port of al-Mahdiya failed when most of the crusaders accepted the terms that the defenders offered. Disease and lack of victuals were among the factors that persuaded them to depart.

Another possibility is to fight the Turks in the Balkans. King Sigismund of Hungary did much in the early 1390s to try to bring the forces of Christendom together to meet the Turkish threat, but in the event the expedition that set out in 1395 was largely limited to French and Burgundian forces, as well as Sigismund's own troops. The problem with crusading against the Ottoman Turks is that they are very formidable warriors. The crusading army was duly humbled in 1396 by Murad I's successor Bāyazîd at Nicopolis, close to the Danube.

You might even think about entering the service of a Muslim ruler, as Chaucer's knight did:

> *This same worthy knight had also been*
> *At some time with the lord of Palatia*
> *Against another heathen in Turkey.*

So, rather surprisingly, did Boucicaut, who was with Sultan Murad I for three months in 1388. He hoped that this would lead to expeditions against other Muslims, but was disappointed.

OPPOSITE *The crusading expedition commanded by the duke of Bourbon sailing to al-Mahdiya in 1390.*

Spain

The sensible advice, not that anyone in this period is prepared to say it, is not to mess with the Mamluks or tangle with the Turks. There are alternatives for the crusading knight. In Spain, the Moors have been in retreat for many years as the kingdoms of Aragon, Castile and Portugal have expanded. If you go to Spain, you will be surprised at the extent to which Moorish habits have been adopted in the Christian kingdoms. There is a cultural mix, and you may be startled to find, for example, that there are so many public baths in Spanish cities. The Emirate of Granada is still Muslim, and is an obvious target for crusades.

There are notable examples of crusades in Spain. As he was dying, Robert Bruce, king of Scots, said that he wanted his heart taken on crusade, and it was to Spain that James Douglas duly took it. He carried the heart hanging round his neck in a silver case. The two year-long siege of Algeciras, which fell to the crusaders in 1344, witnessed knights from all over Europe assisting Alfonso XI of Castile; the earls of Derby and Salisbury were there, as was Philip of Navarre, cousin to the French king, and the count of Foix. Chaucer's knight was at Algeciras. There is a real need for knights to fight against the Moors of Granada, but you must remember that they are dangerous opponents, well versed in how to fight crusaders.

The Baltic

An attractive alternative to the Mediterranean world in some ways is the Baltic, and the Papacy is quite happy to grant the full privileges of a crusader to those who fight the pagans here. Expeditions there are a safer and more satisfactory experience than crusading in the Mediterranean, where defeat is all too likely. Boucicaut found an expedition to the Baltic to be 'grand, and very honourable and fine, with a great company of knights, squires and noble men'.

The Baltic is a region of German expansion. The Teutonic Knights are spearheading the drive eastwards. Their order was originally set up to fight in the Holy Land, but their interests were diverted to the Baltic. In 1309 they established their base at Marienburg, after occupying Gdansk in the previous year. A contemporary commentator wrote:

*This order is the Order of the Germans and of Blessed Mary
of the Teutons, because they hardly receive anyone as
a brother unless he is German-speaking.*

The Teutonic Knights established a strong bureaucratic system of government in Prussia, and they are strong in Livonia, but after their defeat by the Poles at Tannenberg in 1410 they are no longer quite the force they were. Their main crusading role is in Lithuania. The Lithuanians are pagan; their ruler Vytautas accepted baptism in 1386, but conversion of the country has barely started. You should not think that this means that they are primitive; their state is well organized, and they are excellent warriors. They have some habits that are difficult to stomach; they go in for polygamy, cremate their dead and regard some trees as holy. The Teutonic Knights need help in fighting what appears to be an endless war against them.

Crusading journeys, or *Reisen*, are run with true German efficiency. The Teutonic Knights know what you want; you could think of a *Reise* as a package crusade. There will be outdoor feasts, hunting and jousting to enjoy, and there is always the pleasing expectation that there will be pagans to kill. The forests are full of ermines and sables, so you should be able to buy a fine fur coat. To get to the Baltic you should go

*A 14th-century German knight.
Expansion into the Baltic lands is
the major crusading activity for the
Germans, under the leadership of
the Teutonic Knights.*

113

by sea to Marienburg or perhaps Königsberg; that is easier than the land route. From there, the Teutonic Knights will organize your transport on to Lithuania. You can choose between a winter and a summer expedition. In winter it is very, very cold, and you can ride fast on the frozen land; in summer you have to hope for heat to dry out the swampy territory.

A lot of knights go on the journeys to the Baltic. The Germans are in the great majority, but there are significant numbers from other parts of Christendom. In the winter of 1367–68, 97 Englishmen received permission to go to Prussia. A great many French knights have undertaken the expedition there. Boucicaut, indeed, went three times to fight the pagans in Lithuania. One of his journeys was in winter. The enemy were pursued for eight days, and on their return to Marienburg the crusaders were treated to a grand dinner. Twelve knights, from different countries, were selected to sit at the high table; Boucicaut was probably rather put out not to be one of them.

Henry Bolingbroke, the future English king Henry IV, went on two *Reisen* to the Baltic. He was involved in heavy fighting at the siege of Vilnius on his first expedition in 1390–91, but these were enjoyable trips, with a great deal of food and drink available. The fact that a crusade is a religious enterprise does not seem to have bothered Henry much; he spent more on gambling than he did on almsgiving. There is one problem, however, attractive as a cruise on the Baltic with a bit of warfare thrown in may appear. You will almost certainly be out of pocket. There is not much booty to be had, and anything you do take is likely to be grabbed by the Teutonic Knights.

A crusading knight at prayer. Religious motivation is at the heart of the crusading movement, but crusaders may also hope to gain fame and even fortune.

OF CRUSADES

In 1390 Henry Bolingbroke took 13 knights, 18 squires, 3 heralds, 10 miners, 6 minstrels and 60 servants and others on crusade in the Baltic lands.

✠

Lithuanians worship many gods; Percunos is the god of fire and lightning, Potrimpo the god of fertility and rivers, and Picollos the god of the underworld.

Count William IV of Holland went on seven crusading expeditions in the Baltic.

✠

The sultan Bāyazîd, having defeated the crusaders at Nicopolis, was himself defeated by the Mongolian ruler Timur (also known as Tamerlane) in 1402 and was taken prisoner.

A grand tour

Crusading offers a lot if what you really want is travel. Henry Bolingbroke's second expedition, in 1392–93, shows the excellent tour you can do by combining crusade and pilgrimage:

- ✠ Start at Gdansk, and go to Königsberg and back.

- ✠ Then set off southwards, to Frankfurt an der Oder.

- ✠ Travel to Bohemia to see Prague, and the great castle at Karlstejn.

- ✠ Vienna is the next major stop, followed by Klagenfurt.

- ✠ Cross the Alps, which should not be too difficult.

- ✠ Next, aim for Venice. It's a good idea to spend a few days on the Lido, as well as in the city itself.

- ✠ From Venice take ship to the Holy Land, and make a pilgrimage to Jerusalem.

- ✠ On your return, visit Cyprus, Rhodes and the Greek mainland, before returning to Italy.

When he did it, the whole trip took Henry a year, and if you can afford it, it will be a wonderful experience. You might even be able to bring back, as Henry did, a leopard and a parrot as mementos of the journey. Don't get too excited, though, about what you will see in distant lands; you will not be going to those far-off places inhabited by headless men who have faces in their chests, or the countries where the people have dog's heads, or just one leg with one giant foot, which they use as a sunshade.

Crusades against Christians

There is one more possibility for you as a crusader. It may surprise you to learn that you can go on crusade against other Christians. In 1378 there was a double election, with Urban VI in Rome claiming to be pope, and his rival Clement VII in Avignon arguing that the title was his. In 1383 the bishop of Norwich, who had some experience of fighting in Italy, led a crusade to Flanders against Clement's supporters, which achieved nothing save his disgrace. Both popes were ready to offer crusading privileges to those who would fight for their cause. At the battle of Aljubarrota in 1385 the Castilians were crusading for Clement, and the Portuguese with their English allies were doing the same for Urban.

Do you have to go?

Of course it is not compulsory for a knight to go on crusade. John Hawkwood was among those who never did so. Surprisingly, Geoffroi de Charny does not recommend that you should do so, perhaps because his own experience on crusade was unsatisfactory. It will, however, add to your reputation if you do join a crusading expedition, and it should help you to attain salvation. It is difficult to advise you where would be best to go. As previously noted, it would be sensible to avoid fighting the Turks or Mamluks, and the fact that there are 110 different types of biting midges in Lithuania is a little worrying, not to mention the horseflies. It is, however, surely too unadventurous to crusade against fellow Christians in the Low Countries. The best answer is perhaps Spain, but the choice is up to you.

ꟽERCEꟼARIES

*If you do not make these payments as you are obliged by
promises and pacts, you will have to excuse us that we also
do not obey the pacts between ourselves and your commune.*

JOHN THORNBURY TO THE CITIZENS OF SIENA, 1375

‡   ‡   ‡

 t is hardly unreasonable to expect to be paid, whatever sort of
knight you are. Being a mercenary, however, is more than just
a matter of taking pay. If you are willing to take money from
any employer, and to change sides if the money is right, then
you are a mercenary, and there are some good opportunities awaiting you.
This is a career for professional soldiers, and you need to be aware that you
are as likely to gain notoriety as fame. If you are a German knight, above all
from Swabia or the Rhineland, then the temptation to go to fight as a mercenary in Italy is particularly strong.

You might expect the experts to regard this kind of career as the contra-
diction of all that is chivalric, but Geoffroi de Charny is far from hostile to
it. He discusses knights who leave their homeland and go to Italy, and his
conclusion is that they deserve considerable praise.

> *Through this they can see, learn and gain knowledge of much that
> is good through participating in war, for they may be in such
> lands or territories where they can witness and themselves achieve
> great feats of arms.*

Geoffroi's warning is that those who do take this course should not be
tempted to give it up too soon, taking a quick profit. He says that even when
the body can do no more, your heart and will should drive you on.

Origins

A career as a mercenary is particularly tempting if you are not quite from the top drawer. This is a route to take if you are looking to make your way in the world, and are prepared to take considerable risks. Few of the English mercenary captains had noble or knightly backgrounds. John Hawkwood's origins lay in an Essex village; he was the second son of a minor landholder. Some of the Gascons come from minor noble families, as is also the case with many of the Germans. Werner of Urslingen was exceptional in being of high-born ancestry, for he was a younger son of Duke Conrad VI von Urslingen, and claimed the title of Duke of Spoleto. When they are in Italy, some Germans claim titles that they are not really entitled to, and many of them are knighted on campaign there. So do not worry that if you fight as a mercenary you will be lowered in status. The contrary is far more likely to be the case.

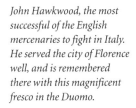

John Hawkwood, the most successful of the English mercenaries to fight in Italy. He served the city of Florence well, and is remembered there with this magnificent fresco in the Duomo.

Opportunities

Italy presents the richest pickings for you in your career as a mercenary. The rivalries between the cities of the north lead to much fighting, and these cities are so wealthy that they can afford to hire the best soldiers from Germany, England and elsewhere. Peace does not present much of a problem; there is always another conflict and another city ready to recruit you. Florence is always opposed to Siena; Milan has numerous enemies.

The companies

To be a successful mercenary you need to be a part of, or preferably lead, a company. The first of these in the 14th century was the Catalan Grand Company of Roger of Flor, formed in 1302 from veterans of the Aragonese army that had been fighting in Sicily. The Company began by serving the Byzantine emperor, but soon started to operate independently, causing chaos in Greece, capturing Athens, and setting an example of destructive behaviour for others to follow.

The Germans

Next came the Germans. When the German emperor Henry VII died in Italy in 1313, his army was dissolved, and many of his knights remained in Italy to seek their fortunes. Ludwig IV's journey to Rome in 1327 took more knights there, and as Ludwig could not pay their wages, many did not return to Germany with him. The first really large mercenary band in Italy, the Company of St George, was founded in 1339, with a leading role taken by Werner of Urslingen. It was defeated by a Milanese army on a snow-covered battlefield at Parabiago, near Milan, but Werner formed a new Great Company in 1342, which ravaged its way through northern Italy until the Germans returned home, much the richer. Werner returned again in 1347, remaining until 1351. He wore black armour, on which his motto was inscribed: 'Enemy of God, Pity and Mercy'.

The Great Company Werner founded had various leaders after him, first Montreal d'Albano, who came from Provence and was known as Fra Moriale, and then the German Conrad of Landau. By the mid-14th century there were at least 3,500 German mercenaries in Italy. Many Germans go to Italy for a single campaigning season; to go for more than three or four campaigns is rare. There are exceptions:

✝ Haneken Bongard spent a quarter of a century in Italy.

✝ Conrad count of Aichelberg spent 15 years there.

Swabians and Rhinelanders normally look to Milan and Tuscany for employment; Bavarians and Franconians gravitate towards Venice.

The English and Gascons

The treaty of 1360 that resolved, for a time, the war between England and France left large numbers of soldiers unemployed. For some the solution to this problem lay in forming free companies, bands known as *routiers*. The leaders of the new companies were mostly English or Gascon. One of the largest, the Great Company, took Pont-Saint-Esprit in the Rhone valley in 1360, using it as a base for launching devastating raids. In 1362 a *routier* force defeated a French royal army at Brignais. One of the most notable bands at this time was the White Company. It sprang from the Great Company and was initially led by a German, Albert Sterz; he was replaced by Hugh Mortimer of La Zouche, a kinsman of the king of England. The White Company was well organized, with a command structure of 12 corporals. It was invited to Italy by the marquis of Montferrat, and in 1363 defeated Conrad of Landau's troops.

This is a world of fluctuating allegiances; you will find that you are playing politics as the companies disintegrate and reform.

- ✝ Sterz and his compatriot Haneken Bongard left the White Company and formed the Company of the Star in 1364.

- ✝ In 1365 the men of the Star defeated and destroyed the White Company, many of whose former members joined John Hawkwood in the Company of St George.

- ✝ Under Hawkwood, many of the English knights in Italy came together in a new company in the early 1370s. This was said to be 10 miles long as it ravaged its way through the Italian countryside.

The companies can present a serious problem; if the mercenaries are not employed by a city, perhaps during a period of truce, they act independently, extorting money where they can, and bringing terror to the land. Nowadays, however, the number of foreign mercenaries in Italy has declined. The glory days of the companies were in the 14th century. Nevertheless, there are many opportunities for you. The great Italian cities will always need to hire experienced mercenaries.

The Italians

You do not have to be a foreigner such as Hawkwood to succeed as a mercenary in Italy, though it may help. Recently Italians, notably Alberigo da
Barbiano, who died in 1409, have come to take much more of a leading role
in the mercenary companies, although there are still plenty of opportunities for foreign knights. There are earlier examples of important Italian
mercenaries:

✝ Guidoriccio da Fogliano came from a noble family in Reggio
   Emilia. He led Siena's army from 1327 to 1334, served the Della
   Scala family in Verona, and joined forces for a time with Werner
   of Urslingen. He has been made famous for posterity by a fresco
   in Siena.

*The Italian mercenary
Guidoriccio da Fogliano
commanding Siena's
army in 1328, painted
by Simone Martini.
His horse is shown
pacing, a movement
in which the legs on
one side move forward
together, followed by
those on the other side.*

✝ Ambrogio Visconti was another notable Italian mercenary.
   He was the bastard son of Bernabò Visconti of Milan, and
   as such could not hope to receive a worthwhile inheritance.
   He sought his fortune in war, founded a new Company of
   St George in 1365, and fought alongside John Hawkwood.

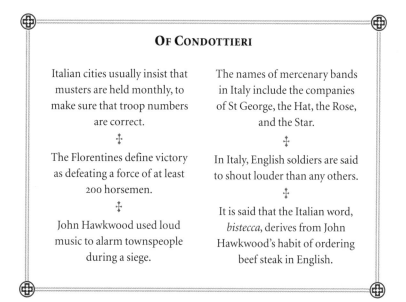

OF CONDOTTIERI

Italian cities usually insist that musters are held monthly, to make sure that troop numbers are correct.

✝

The Florentines define victory as defeating a force of at least 200 horsemen.

✝

John Hawkwood used loud music to alarm townspeople during a siege.

The names of mercenary bands in Italy include the companies of St George, the Hat, the Rose, and the Star.

✝

In Italy, English soldiers are said to shout louder than any others.

✝

It is said that the Italian word, *bistecca*, derives from John Hawkwood's habit of ordering beef steak in English.

Organization

You should make sure that the company you join is well organized. A typical company should have the following:

- ✝ A captain-general.
- ✝ A chancellor, normally Italian, to look after the legal affairs, such as negotiating contracts and drawing up documents.
- ✝ A treasurer to look after the finances.
- ✝ Marshals and constables to command the banners, which will normally consist of 15–20 men.
- ✝ *Guastatori*, the devastators, who do the job of ravaging the countryside.
- ✝ Women to do the laundry, grind corn with hand-mills, cook and provide other services.

OPPOSITE *A group of dismounted men-at-arms, ready for battle.*

Tactics

The methods of the English mercenaries are the best to follow. They have introduced new fighting techniques to Italy. The basic fighting unit employed by the Germans was the *barbuta*, composed of two men, a knight and a page (the latter in support). The English introduced the formation known as the lance to Italy; this has three men – knight, squire and page – and became the standard component by the end of the 14th century. The men of the celebrated English White Company fought on foot, two men holding a single lance, advancing carefully in small steps. Archers provided support to this solid formation. As important as these techniques is the ability to march long distances, often at night. The English troops would appear, apparently from nowhere, to launch surprise attacks on towns and castles using ingenious scaling ladders. Under Hawkwood's command their operations were well planned and properly co-ordinated, as well as being based on sound intelligence; his is the model to follow.

The battle of Castagnaro in 1387 provides a good demonstration of how to fight. Hawkwood was serving the city of Padua, when his small army was pursued by a much larger army from Verona. He established a strong

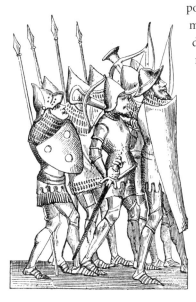

position, protected by ditches and marshes. He also took care to fill a ditch at a vital point, providing a route around the Veronese position. Most of his men-at-arms dismounted, and were drawn up in three lines; his archers were in support, and he kept a cavalry reserve. He countered a frontal attack by the Veronese by outflanking them, and attacked their rear with his mounted knights and men-at-arms. The similarity to the tactics used by the English in France is obvious, with parallels in particular to the battle of Poitiers.

Language difficulties

You need to have some language skills if you are to succeed as a mercenary; it will not be enough to let your sword speak for you. Albert Sterz, originally from Germany, was fluent in English. Conrad of Landau, on the other hand, had problems. He was defeated in 1363, in part because he could not communicate properly with the Hungarians in his company. 'Alt, alt', he shouted at them, but they would not halt. Provided that you have some knowledge of French, you should be able to pick up Italian, something that the Germans find very hard. Ideally, you should know Latin, but John Hawkwood did not, and managed very well by using clerks and notaries.

Negotiations

A successful mercenary needs many skills; it is not enough just to be good at fighting. You will have to negotiate with your employers, and Italians are the best businessmen in the world, so it won't be easy. It is probably fairly easy to agree on the rate of pay, but it is when it comes to the extras that it gets interesting. A good strategy is to insist that you are paid for non-existent soldiers – known as 'dead lances'. As much as 10 per cent of your troop can consist of these ghostly warriors. It is probably a good idea to settle for a lump sum as compensation for lost horses; that way you will not have to prove that the horses really have been killed. In addition to these charges, you can usually extort bribes from cities anxious for your services. You need to watch your employer though; the Italians have a nasty habit of imposing taxes on your pay, and income after tax is rarely as much as you thought it was going to be.

Chivalry

It may seem that few of the knightly virtues are apparent in the attitude of the mercenaries. The German Conrad of Landau put it clearly:

> *It is our custom to rob, sack and kill he who resists. Our income is derived from the funds of the provinces we invade: he who values his life pays for peace and quiet from us a very steep price.*

There is, however, much that is contradictory in the chivalric code, meaning that, conveniently, it can be used to justify the apparently unacceptable, such as:

✝ The ravaging of the countryside.

✝ The levying of protection money.

✝ The seizure of food supplies and the driving off of animals.

✝ The slaughter that follows the successful storming of a town.

These are common elements in warfare today, and are warranted by the laws of war. They do not necessarily stand in opposition to the ideas of chivalry, ideas which have a useful flexibility to them. The actions of a mercenary such as Hawkwood are not necessarily any less chivalrous than those of the Black Prince. The latter's troops were responsible for massacring the inhabitants of Limoges in 1370; Hawkwood's men were among those who took part in the killing at Cesena in 1377. It was, however, Cardinal Robert of Geneva, not Hawkwood, who demanded 'blood and justice' at Cesena. The horrific events there did not dent Hawkwood's chivalric reputation.

If you display valour in fighting, show due loyalty by adhering to the terms of the contracts you make with your employers, and display generosity to your followers, you will be fulfilling your obligations as a knight. It is important that you should conduct yourself in accordance with the accepted laws of war; if you go against these conventions, you will find yourself deprived of such protection as those conventions offer. Hawkwood may not have done all that is expected of a chivalrous knight; he never, for example, went on crusade, and he fathered illegitimate children. He was, however, brave, loyal, and a superb soldier, and as a result has a fine reputation as a chivalric hero.

LADIES & DAMSELS

When we are in taverns, drinking strong wine, and the ladies
are near, looking at us, drawing their kerchiefs round their
smooth necks, their grey eyes smiling, resplendent with
beauty, nature provokes us in our hearts to fight.

THE VOWS OF THE HERON, MID-14TH CENTURY

✠   ✠   ✠

hivalric culture makes much of women. They should be an inspiration for knights. They will be there to cheer you on in tournaments and jousts. Their encouragement will help to persuade you to go off to fight. Should you have doubts about why you are fighting, just think of your lady-love, and try to fulfil her dreams for you. Read Geoffroi de Charny, and he will tell you that you should love, protect and honour all women who inspire knights and men-at-arms to undertake worthy deeds. In reality it is, however, all rather more complicated than that.

Good or evil?

If you listen to some priests, you will gather that women are wicked creatures, who are just after one thing. The early Christian fathers provide good ammunition for such opinions, describing woman as 'a temple built over a sewer'. According to this tradition women are imperfect beings as compared to men. Current medical opinion backs this up:

✠ Women have a different balance of the humours from men. They are colder and have more phlegm, and as a result are fickle and unreliable.

126

- ✝ Women are more sexually voracious than men.
- ✝ Female anatomy is strange, for women have a womb that wanders about the body. This can cause them considerable problems.
- ✝ Women have testicles, but in contrast to men's, these are small, and hidden internally.

However, the cult of the Virgin Mary leads to very different conclusions about women, as do the ideas about courtly love that have been developing since the 12th century. Love in this tradition is a pure emotion; sex does not come into it.

- ✝ Women are to be adored, protected and honoured.
- ✝ Women are merciful; they intercede to seek pardons.
- ✝ They are pious and virtuous.

You will find a range of ideas about women in the stories that you read and hear, but you will normally find them depicted in ideal terms. The perfect woman has a white skin, golden hair, an elegant nose, a mouth well made for kissing, and a perfect figure. Even her toes will be just right.

A lady and her maid, from the Luttrell Psalter *of about 1340. The maid is holding up a mirror so that her lady can admire the way in which her long blonde hair is plaited. Women spend a lot of time like this, ensuring that they look as beautiful as possible.*

A love poem about the fair maid of Ribblesdale provides a description of such a maiden:

> *Her eyes are large and grey, and she,*
> *When darting lovely looks at me,*
> *Arches her brows with light.*
> *The moon that stands in heaven's height*
> *Sheds not such radiance at night.*

The poem is, however, an elaborate joke, for it goes on to say that the maid also has an extraordinarily long neck, like a swan, over 9 inches long, and arms an ell in length, almost 4 feet. The message is clear; you should not take all these descriptions too seriously.

Respect and protect

Chivalric doctrine is clear about the fact that you must respect women. De Charny explains how important it is that you protect your lady-love's honour. You should not boast of your love for her, or behave in such a way that it becomes public knowledge; otherwise you may embarrass her, causing trouble. When Boucicaut was at court, he was gracious, courteous and entirely proper in his demeanour; no one could even tell from his behaviour which lady was the one he loved. If you must kiss women, note the example of Henry of Grosmont, the duke of Lancaster. He found that beautiful ladies of rank disapproved of this, and so he gallantly directed his behaviour towards those of lower classes.

As a good knight, you should protect women from harm. Your concern will primarily be with women of your own social class; when Boucicaut created his order of the White Lady on a Green Shield, he was concerned only with ladies of noble lineage. You may well not worry too much about what happens to peasant women in war, but you should look after aristocratic ladies. There are examples to follow:

✝ John Hawkwood is said to have saved 1,000 women from
   a dreadful fate at the horrific massacre at Cesena in 1377.

A group of knights and ladies in fashionable dress. The ladies wear long flowing gowns with a wide neckline.

✢ In 1358 the rebellious French peasants in the rising known as the *Jacquerie* were threatening a number of noblewomen who had taken refuge in the town of Meaux. The count of Foix and Jean de Grailly (known as the Captal de Buch) drove the peasants off and slaughtered them.

✢ At the taking of Caen in 1346, Thomas Holland and his companions are said to have saved many women and maidens from a dreadful fate; but unfortunately they were unable to do the same for the nuns of the abbey of the Trinity.

It may seem obvious to you that women should be treated properly, but this has not always been the case. When Edward I captured Robert Bruce's sister and the countess of Buchan in 1306 the two women were not sent off to nunneries in England as might have been expected. Instead, cages were constructed for them, and they were placed in full public view, one at Roxburgh, and one at Berwick. The fact that the cages were fitted with en-suite facilities hardly excuses Edward's action, but curiously no one accused him of being unchivalrous. There is a tale doing the rounds about Edward III, king of England, who is said to have raped the countess of Salisbury. This, however, you should not believe; the names, dates and places simply do not add up. Edward was a chivalrous man.

Vows and tokens of affection

In Armorica, that is called Britain,
There was a knight that loved, and put all his pain
To serve a lady in his best wise.
And many a labour, many a great enterprise
He wrought for his lady, before she was won.
For she was the fairest under the sun.
CHAUCER, FROM *THE FRANKLIN'S TALE*

It is often their wives and girlfriends who persuade knights to make vows to perform valiant deeds in war. You may find that your loved one gives you a token, such as a detachable sleeve, for you to tie to your helmet or your lance; in return you will be expected to perform noble deeds in her name. William Marmion's lady-love chose to give him a gilded crest for his helmet, and instructed him to make it famous in the most dangerous place in Britain. Marmion duly set off in an act of devotion, and was almost killed for his pains at the siege of Norham Castle.

Ladies sometimes use questionable methods of persuasion. When the Scots captured Douglas Castle early in the 14th century, they found a

A Burgundian ceremonial shield, depicting a knight making a vow to his lady. The motto in a scroll reads 'You or death'. A skeleton behind the knight suggests that death will be the outcome.

letter on the body of the constable, in which his girlfriend promised to sur-render herself to him once he had managed to keep the castle secure for a year. If you are offered a bargain along such lines, ask yourself whether the lady really means it. She may just be looking for a way to get rid of an unwanted suitor, by sending you off into danger.

At the start of Edward III's war with France, a great banquet was held, at which the centrepiece was a roast heron. According to a poem about the event, *The Vows of the Heron*, all present took vows to perform notable actions in the fighting that was to come. The beautiful daughter of the earl of Derby placed a finger over one of the earl of Salisbury's eyes, and he swore not to open it again until he had set fire to the French countryside and fought against Philip VI's army. The poem makes fun of the practice. Salisbury had already lost the sight in one eye, and was either agreeing to go to war blind, or making a meaningless vow. Although this is a satirical account, it is the case that a number of young men went to war in the late 1330s wearing eyepatches in fulfilment of promises they made. This was not sensible, and the girlfriends who persuaded them to do this should have known better.

You do not need to make impractical or dangerous vows, and you should ditch the object of your affection if she tries to get you to do so. You can find more sensible women. Elizabeth de Juliers, niece of the English queen Philippa and wealthy widow of the earl of Kent, fell in love with Eustace d'Auberchicourt. She took a wise view of what a knight needs, and provided practical help as well as symbols of devotion. While he was fight-ing in Champagne, 'she sent him several hackneys and chargers, with love-letters and other tokens of great affection, by which the knight was inspired to still greater feats of bravery and accomplished such deeds that everyone talked of him.'

Tournaments

Women have a big part to play in all the events that surround tournaments, and you will have an enjoyable time playing court to them, flirting in, no doubt, the most proper way. The ladies lead the knights in processions, they fill the spectator stands, cheer their favourite champion, and enjoy the dinners and the dances. At the London event of 1390, there were even prizes for them, as the general invitation to the jousts explained:

> *And the lady or damsel who dances best or leads the most joyful life*
> *those three days aforesaid, that is to say Sunday, Monday and*
> *Tuesday, will be given a golden brooch by the knights. And the lady*
> *who dances and revels best after her, which is to say the second prize*
> *for those three days, will be given a ring of gold with a diamond.*

The example of a German 13th-century tournament in Magdeburg, in which a woman was offered as the prize, is not one that should be followed. Beware, too, lest the excitements of the tournament lead women to go too far. There is a story of a group of eye-catching young ladies in England, some 40 or 50 in number, who took to dressing as men, and appearing on fine horses at tournaments. They also, to the disapproval of the chronicler Henry Knighton, but no doubt to the delight of the onlookers, 'wantonly and licentiously displayed their bodies in a scurrilous manner'.

Marriage: a tale of two Constances

In planning your career, you should think hard about what sort of marriage you should enter into. The right wife will provide you with the support that you need in your military career. Marry wealth, and you will have the resources you need to meet all the costs involved in war. Marry unwisely, and you will face problems and distractions that you could do without.

Hugh Calveley provides a cautionary note. In 1368 he married Constança, daughter of a Sicilian noble and one of the queen of Aragon's ladies. She brought a substantial dowry with her, but if she was initially pleased at the prospect of marriage to a hero of the Anglo-French war, her pleasure soon palled. The marriage was childless, and Constança refused to leave her estates in Valencia to join Calveley, becoming instead the mistress of Pedro IV's son Juan.

In contrast, Calveley's companion-in-arms Robert Knollys had a highly successful marriage. He did not seek a bride with a fortune, or an exotic foreign beauty. His Constance hailed from Yorkshire, and was a woman of character rather than wealth. She met Robert in Brittany, where she had been taking an active part in the war, even leading contingents of troops. She frequently accompanied her husband on his expeditions, taking their children with her. It is, one need hardly add, highly unusual for a woman to take part in war in this way.

The best advice is to pursue one of the following courses of action:

✛ Find a wife like Constance Knollys, who will share your experiences to the full.

✛ Follow the example of Eustace d'Auberchicourt, and find a wealthy widow who loves you.

✛ Marry someone capable of running your affairs; John Hawkwood's Italian wife Donnina was highly literate and was a good businesswoman.

You ought to pay more attention to your lover than to your falcon. The German knight Konrad of Altstetten's lady-love is shown in the early 14th century Codex Manesse *trying to distract his attention while he feeds his bird.*

OF LADIES

In 1338 Agnes, Countess of Dunbar, successfully defended her castle for 19 weeks.

✠

The French doctor Henri de Mondeville suggests that if well-endowed young women are reluctant to undergo cosmetic surgery, they can wear shirts fitted with two appropriately shaped bags so as to provide support.

✠

The English knight Thomas Murdak was murdered by his wife in 1316; she and her associates chopped him in half.

Some of Richard II of England's knights were accused of paying too much attention to women, 'showing more prowess in the bedroom than on the field of battle, defending themselves more with their tongue than with their lance.'

✠

In 1386 the Paduan army captured 211 prostitutes when they defeated an army from Verona. They were treated very honourably, and dined with the lord of Padua.

Trouble

It may be the case, as de Charny and others would argue, that devotion to a lady inspires you to do great things on campaign and on the battlefield. However, you should sometimes take a reality check on these romantic ideals; women may cause you problems. Take the case of William Gold, who served in Italy alongside John Hawkwood. Gold acquired a French mistress, called Janet, who failed to tell him that she already had a husband. She ran off, taking some of his money. William was heartbroken, and wrote about it in dramatic terms:

> *Love overcometh all things, since it prostrates even the stout, making them impatient, taking all heart from them, even casting down into the depths the summit of tall towers, suggesting strife, so that it drags them into deadly duel, as has happened to and befallen me for the sake of this Janet, my heart yearning so towards her.*

All the efforts he made to get Janet back distracted Gold from the business of war, rather than inspiring him to perform great deeds of valour. Eventually he forgot Janet, and without womanly distractions served the city of Venice so well that he was made a citizen.

You will find nothing in the pages of Geoffroi de Charny's work to suggest that your lady-love will be anything other than loyal and devoted. Do not believe all that you read. You may well be worried about what she is doing in your absence, and you could be right to be concerned. In 1303 William Latimer, one of Edward I's household knights, went to the king when they were campaigning in Scotland to complain that he had heard that his wife had been abducted, and that she had gone willingly. The king was furious, and demanded that some legal remedy be worked out. Latimer was eventually given full powers to arrest his wife and get her back, but by then she was safely ensconced as the mistress of another knight, Nicholas Meinill, and though in time she would leave him too, she never returned to Latimer.

The chronicler Froissart was told a story about two brothers-in-arms, Louis Raimbaut and Limousin. Raimbaut had a mistress of whom he was inordinately fond, and when he was away campaigning, he entrusted her to Limousin. However, he did rather more than look after her, and the gossip duly reached Raimbaut, who had Limousin stripped near naked, marched through the town and publicly beaten. Raimbaut was later captured, to be taunted by Limousin: 'One woman might have served two brothers-in-arms, such as we were then.' That is not a good idea for you to follow up.

Boucicaut never allowed his eyes to stray, but it may be too much to hope that you will be able to follow his example of chivalric morality. What should you do with the outcome of illicit liaisons? Walter Mauny had two illegitimate daughters, Maloisel and Malplesant, and packed them off to a nunnery. When John de Warenne, earl of Surrey, discarded his mistress, he sent his two sons by her away to become knights of the Hospital. In contrast, John Hawkwood looked after his illegitimate children. His son Thomas became a soldier, and distinguished himself in the Anglo-French war, while Hawkwood used his influence with the Papacy to secure a career in the church for another son, John. This is surely the example to follow.

✧ XII ✧

Sïege

*However much our guns impaired the defences of the barbican or
the walls and towers by day, by night the enemy made good the
damage on top of the barbican and walls with timber, fascines,
and tubs filled with earth, dung, sand or stones.*

GESTA HENRICI QUINTI, 1415

✧   ✧   ✧

 nights are not particularly good at sieges, for lance and sword
are of little use when faced with walls of stone and ramparts of
earth. Yet you will find that much of your time campaigning
will be spent camped in front of a castle or town, awaiting its
surrender. Alternatively, you may be a member of a garrison, defending the
walls against attack. Siege warfare is for the most part slow and deliberate,
as each side tries to cancel out the other's advantage; there will be moments
of explosive action, with an assault or a sally. There are conventions governing
the way in which a siege should be conducted, from the formal
challenge at the outset, to the eventual surrender.

Assault

You will probably be anxious to launch a direct assault on any castle or
town that you besiege. Do not attempt this without proper equipment. At
the English siege of the small Scottish castle of Caerlaverock in 1300, the
common soldiers rushed towards the walls, and were driven back as the

OPPOSITE *Caerlaverock Castle in southwestern Scotland was successfully besieged
by Edward I of England in 1300. The castle has an unusual triangular plan.*

136

garrison hurled stones and shot at them. Then the knights attacked. This
was described in *The Song of Caerlaverock*:

> *Many ran there, many leaped there, and many used such haste to go,*
> *that they did not deign to speak to any one. Then might there be seen*
> *such kind of stones thrown as if they would beat hats and helmets to*
> *powder, and break shields and targets in pieces; for to kill and*
> *wound was the game at which they played. Great shouts arose*
> *among them, when they perceived that any mischief occurred.*

One group was particularly foolish, pushing forward towards the castle
with no thought for their safety, and with no chance of breaking through
the defences:

> *These did not act like discreet people, nor as persons enlightened by*
> *understanding; but as if they had been inflamed and blinded with*
> *pride and despair, for they made their way right forwards to the*
> *very brink of the ditch.*

Shields were shattered, and men were bruised and exhausted. The
assault was pointless.

This illustration from a manuscript of The Travels of Marco Polo *shows the use of scaling ladders to assault a town.*

If you must make a direct assault, you will do better if you have scaling ladders or some other means of reaching the top of the walls, though this is risky and is not strongly recommended. When Boucicaut was besieging a castle near Constantinople in 1399, two scaling ladders were erected, only for the defenders to break them with missiles. Then Boucicaut ordered the construction of a stouter ladder from two ship's masts. The first knight up fought valiantly, but was disarmed; a squire following next forced his way onto the ramparts, and 10 or 12 men followed, before the ladder broke. They were rescued only because some of their comrades had forced their way into the castle through a mine.

Cunning plans

You do not want to get involved in a long siege. It can become extremely tedious, and conditions are not likely to be good. Surprise attacks are an excellent alternative. The Scots proved masters at this type of warfare when they took English castle after English castle in the early 14th century. On one occasion, they hid men inside a wagonload of hay, and as the wagon was being driven through the castle gate, the traces were cut, leaving the gate open. To the surprise of the garrison, the Scots leaped out from the hay, and their comrades outside the castle rushed in. Another time the Scots mounted a successful night assault on another castle by going on all fours, mooing like cows, and totally deceiving the (clearly rather foolish) watchmen.

Edinburgh fell in 1314 because one of the Scots knew a way to climb the rock on which the castle stands. As a young man, he had been a member of the garrison, and learned this route so as to visit his girlfriend in the town. When the time came, the Scots mounted a diversionary attack on the main gate of the castle, while a party scaled the rock and forced their way in.

It is not just the Scots who are adept at outwitting the enemy. Bertrand du Guesclin used surprise tactics similar to those of the Scots when as a young man he took the castle of Fougeray by disguising himself and his men as woodcutters. A Gascon soldier, the Bascot de Mauléon, was successful when he disguised himself and his companions as women carrying water into a castle. You may think that it is unchivalric to use tricks such as these, but if you are successful, you are unlikely to be criticized for it.

Mining

You can employ miners to dig, so as to bring down castle walls, and even to force an entry to a castle. It can, however, take a long time to construct a mine, particularly if the ground is hard and rocky.

When the duke of Bourbon besieged the castle of Vertueil on the river Charente in 1385 there was much discussion as to whether the best means of attack was by scaling ladders or a mine. After reconnoitring the site on horseback, the duke decided on mining. The castle was on a rocky site, and the excavation took six weeks. Royal orders instructing the duke to go to

Flanders presented him with a major problem; it would be dishonourable to leave the siege, but equally dishonourable to disobey royal instructions. Haste was needed. The king sent more money, and the duke doubled the number of miners. When the mine was ready, the duke himself entered it. The commander of the defenders, Montferrand, was so overcome at being opposed by someone of such rank that he promptly offered surrender. The agreement included a remarkable provision that a number of the attackers (who included Boucicaut in their number) should fight the defenders, one by one, in the darkness of the mine tunnel. After this was done, the formal ceremony of surrender took place. Montferrand went on his knees before the duke, and promised to serve him as his man. That, at least, is the account in the life of the duke; Boucicaut's *Life* tells of a breach in the walls made by the mine, with its hero one of the first to enter, fighting with lance and sword, hand-to-hand, as valiantly as only he could.

Mines can be countered by counter-mines. Henry V tried to undermine the walls of Harfleur, but was twice thwarted by the skill of the besieged, who drove their own mines to block those constructed by the English. When mine and counter-mine meet, there is an opportunity for you, as a knight, to see how you like fighting underground. It is not pleasant.

Bombardment

The best method of reducing a castle is probably to bombard it using siege engines and guns; you will not, however, find that this gives you, as a knight, much to do.

In 1300 at Caerlaverock, after the assaults failed, it was the engineer, Master Robert of Holme, who achieved the breakthrough. He had erected four great stone-throwing machines, trebuchets, which had been brought in disassembled form by sea. Accounts reveal some of the costs:

> *To Simon de Rish, master of the ship St George of Dartmouth, for carriage and windage of two of the king's engines to Caerlaverock, and for the damage done when his ropes were broken by the engines, paid to his own hands at Caerlaverock, 14 July. 6s. 8d.*

The bombardment from the trebuchets was too much for the garrison. Stones rained down on them, shattering as they fell into the courtyard and causing many casualties. Surrender was duly offered. The entire siege lasted no more than a week.

Boucicaut's siege of the count of Périgord's castle of Montignac also shows how effective a bombardment can be. In 1398 Boucicaut marched to the castle with about 1,000 men. Five four-wheeled long carts carried the heavy siege equipment, three carts bore the camping gear, and 200 sumpter horses took the rest of the baggage. To start proceedings, the legal summons to the count was read out; the response came in the form of crossbow bolts. A direct assault achieved nothing; a few men reached the ramparts, only to be thrown down to their deaths. Carpenters and other workmen were recruited; four trebuchets and three *couillards* (see below) were set up. Guns were also trained on the castle. The bombardment lasted for about two months, and finally the count offered to surrender. Boucicaut agreed the terms; the count was promised life and limb, and his men were allowed to leave the castle with their horses and arms. The outcome was satisfactory, but the siege had been a long one, and offered the knights no opportunity to display their skill with arms. As this example shows, it is trebuchets and guns that bring about surrender, not the knights and men-at-arms.

In this picture a couillard *is being prepared, ready to hurl a stone into a castle under siege. The stone can be clearly seen in its sling, about to be released.*

Siege engines

You ought to understand something about siege engines and their capabilities, even though it is the engineers and gunners who operate them, since they have the technical expertise.

The trebuchet

This is the biggest and grandest stone-throwing machine. It works by means of a counterweight at one end of a long beam, with a sling at the other. The beam swivels on a large frame. Because the counterweight is heavy (up to 10 tons is possible), there is a system of ropes and windlasses so that the beam can be hauled down ready to shoot. Trebuchets can hurl stones of 200 or 300 lb a couple of hundred yards. They are accurate, providing that the stones are all the same weight.

The couillard

This is a lighter form of trebuchet. It has two counterweights, and is mounted on a single post; the counterweights swing down on either side of this. The name derives from a slang word for testicles, which the two counterweights resemble.

The springald

This works by using the force of twisted ropes. A solid framework is needed; two bow arms are set in the ropes. A winch or screw is used to haul back the bowstring; the weapon then shoots a large bolt. This is more often used for the defence of

The power of a trebuchet comes from the counterweight. When released, the long beam swings upright, and the stone projectile is whipped out of the sling on a high trajectory.

a castle than for attack. It is powerful; a springald bolt can spear its way through four or five men.

The sow

This is a strong shelter, which can be wheeled up to the walls. A battering ram can be operated under the shelter of a sow, or workmen can hack away at the castle walls with picks.

The belfry

This is a great wooden tower, mounted on wheels, which can be pushed up to the walls of a castle on a carefully prepared trackway. You can then assault the castle from this tower. Edward I of England captured Bothwell castle in 1301 by using a belfry.

ABOVE *A belfry is moved up to a castle, and a drawbridge is lowered to the battlements.*

BELOW, LEFT *Battering rams can breach strong castle walls.*

BELOW, RIGHT *A sow is wheeled up to a castle so that men can attack the walls with picks. The defenders have lowered timbers in front of the walls to provide them with some protection.*

Guns

These are the most modern element in a besieger's armoury. Gunpowder has been used in sieges as an explosive since at least the beginning of the last century, and guns were known in the 1320s. It took a long time before heavy guns capable of battering down walls were developed, and there are considerable problems with them. They take a long time to load; 12 shots a day is a fast rate of fire. They have shown their value in some sieges, but it is impossible to believe that they can ever do more than supplement the trebuchet. You need to be careful with guns; the best advice is to stay well away from them, for they have a tendency to explode in your face.

Although slow to load, bombards can be very effective in sieges. Saltpetre, sulphur and charcoal are used to make the gunpowder for them. They fire stone projectiles with much greater force than even the largest trebuchet, and are capable of bringing down castle walls.

Blockade

One way to capture a town or castle is to blockade it, depriving the occupants of food. If you can, avoid getting involved in this sort of thing. Blockades usually take a long time, and often result in misery for both sides.

✠ At Berwick in 1316 the English garrison were reduced to eating their horses (something the English have always disliked doing). The knights and men-at-arms got the meat, leaving the infantry to gnaw the bones.

OF SIEGE MACHINES

Church roofs are a good source of lead for the trebuchet counterweights.

✝

At the siege of Stirling in 1304, Thomas Gray was struck through the head, below the eyes, by a bolt from a springald, but recovered from the wound.

✝

A necromancer told the duke of Anjou that he could conjure up a bridge from the air, so that he could capture the Castel dell'Ovo in the bay of Naples. The duke did not believe him, and had his head struck off.

The rate of operation for a trebuchet is about three or four stones hurled every hour.

✝

In 1344 at Collioure on the French Mediterranean coast the defenders set up a trebuchet, but miscalculated the weight needed for the counterweight, so that the stone was hurled straight up in the air, falling back down on the engine and breaking it.

✝

The counterweight for a trebuchet can weigh as much as ten tons.

✝ At the king of Aragon's siege of Iglesias in Sardinia, which started in 1323 and lasted over seven months, both sides were severely hit by an epidemic. The townspeople were reduced to eating rats and grass, and when the place finally surrendered early in 1324, there was only one day's food left.

✝ During the siege of Brest in 1373, incessant rain caused major problems. The besieging French had nothing to eat, while the English in the town were forced to devour their horses. The siege failed in the end, as English ships came to the rescue.

✝ Henry V's siege of Harfleur provides another example of the problems that may occur during a blockade. Dysentery struck his army, causing the deaths of the bishop of Norwich and the earl of Suffolk, and killing far more men than the fighting did.

Negotiation

Sieges can be very expensive and take a long time. What you need to do is to negotiate surrender. It is best if you are prepared to allow the defenders of a town or castle some satisfaction, to let them leave feeling that their honour is intact. It is far more difficult if you insist on unconditional surrender, and expect the garrison to make their exit in sackcloth and ashes.

You may be able to pay the garrison off. The English surrendered the castle of St Sauveur in Normandy in 1375 in return for a payment of 53,000 francs. This can create problems; accepting such a sum of money may be seen as dishonourable, and the surrender of St Sauveur was one of the charges brought against William Latimer in parliament in 1376. If you can, try to ensure that all sides come out honourably.

A common agreement is one in which a garrison agrees to surrender after a given period of time, provided no relieving force appears. The battle of Bannockburn was the result of one such arrangement; in 1314 the English in Stirling Castle agreed to surrender provided they were not relieved by midsummer. In the event, the English army appeared in time, but the Scots blocked their final advance on the castle, and then defeated them in battle. The castle duly surrendered. At Iglesias in Sardinia, a deal was struck whereby surrender would take place by 13 February 1324 if no relief came. In fact, desperation led the garrison to give up a week earlier.

Sacking a town or castle

If it proves impossible to negotiate the surrender of a town or castle, then a besieging force is permitted under the law of arms to sack it. This can be a pretty brutal business. The case of the sack of Limoges in 1370 by the Black Prince and his men is particularly notorious. The walls were mined and brought down, and the English burst in, to do their worst. Froissart felt strongly about what happened:

> *There was not that day in the city of Limoges any heart so hardened, or that had any sense of religion, who did not deeply bewail the unfortunate events passing before their eyes; for upwards of three thousand men, women and children were put to death that day.*

In terms of the law, however, the citizens had committed treason against the prince, and Limoges was taken by force. The English were fully entitled to do as they did, though many found it appalling.

Defence

Do not get the idea that a siege is always successful. Sieges of large towns and cities in particular are unlikely to succeed. In their wars in France the English failed to take Tournai in 1340, or Reims in 1359–60. Indeed, the siege of Calais in 1346–47 was their only real success.

You may well find yourself in a castle under siege, as part of the garrison. The methods available to defenders are similar to those employed by besiegers.

- ✣ You can counter an assault with a sally.

- ✣ A counter-mine, carefully dug, will enable you to attack the besieging miners underground.

- ✣ Your own siege engines can be directed at those hurling stones at your castle.

- ✣ Springalds and crossbows can be particularly effective at picking off besiegers.

- ✣ You can even try hooking your enemies up, as if you are fishing for them. This sounds unlikely, but it can work. At the siege of Stirling in 1304 Henry de Beaumont was caught in such a manner, and came close to being dragged into the castle.

Being besieged is not a pleasant experience. You may, however, be able to interrupt the proceedings by challenging one of the besiegers to single combat, and so enhance your reputation for deeds of arms. If your town or castle is under siege, you need to hold out for a reasonable length of time; no one should then accuse you of disloyalty or unchivalrous behaviour if you then surrender. What you should not do is try to hold out to the bitter end; the starvation and misery are not worth it.

✠ XIII ✠

BATTLE

*Banners, forward, forward! Let us take the Lord God as our
protector, and let every man acquit himself honourably.*

THE DUKE OF LANCASTER, ACCORDING TO JOHN CHANDOS'S HERALD, 1367

✠ ✠ ✠

s a valorous knight, you will, of course, want to fight in battle.
For Geoffroi de Charny, battle is the peak of what a knight can
do. Think, however, of the dangers. Before you ride into the
fight, full of a sense of chivalric glory, determined to display
your prowess, remember the scene after the battle of Nicopolis in 1396.
Boucicaut had been captured, and stood in his underclothes before the
Turkish sultan, expecting to be executed along with so many of the Christian army. That is something you want to avoid.

Should you fight?

You should not expect to fight in many major battles. Boucicaut was
involved in just three. If you are sensible, you will see that the risks involved
in battle often outweigh the possible gains. At Buirenfosse in 1339, the
English and their allies faced a French army for a day, but no fighting took
place. The sides were thought to be too easily matched for it to be worth
risking a battle. However, there are those who argue that it is only through
battle that war can be brought to an end. If you take the view that battle is a
form of trial before God, you will want to fight to prove that your side is in
the right. You will find that some commanders are eager to commit their
troops to battle.

- ✠ Edward III's strategy of destroying the French countryside in savage raids was intended to persuade the understandably reluctant Philip VI to fight. Eventually the English king succeeded at Crécy in 1346.

- ✠ The crusaders at Nicopolis in 1396 wanted battle, as they thought they had a divine mission to fight the Turks.

- ✠ The bellicose Henry V was not content in 1415 with capturing the town of Harfleur, but hoped that by marching north he would be able to engage the French, which he did at Agincourt.

The battle of Poitiers in 1356, from a manuscript of Froissart's Chronicles. *This typical battle scene shows the victorious English on the left. English archers are shown shooting at the mounted French vanguard.*

Plan in advance

It is a good idea to think out your battle tactics in advance, and if you are a knight of great distinction, you may have the chance to do so. Before the recent battle of Agincourt in 1415, Boucicaut drew up a plan for battle against the English. There were to be two large battalions, one a vanguard, which could join together to form a single body. Two flanking wings of footsoldiers were to have archers positioned in front of them. A reserve battalion of 1,000 men-at-arms was to be used to attack the English archers, while a smaller reserve of 200 men was to go right round to assault the English baggage train from the rear. In the event, the English were able

to counter these tactics by selecting a narrow field of battle, and the French were unable to deal with the English archers, who protected their positions with stakes.

It is exceptional to have a written plan like Boucicaut's, but though the French failed at Agincourt, advance planning is obviously advisable. There is every indication that the English had their battle plans at Crécy and Poitiers properly thought out in advance; the crusaders at Nicopolis, however, were in disarray and if they had plans, they certainly did not put them into proper effect.

Suitable terrain

Make sure that the terrain is right for the way you want to fight.

- ✠ The boggy ground of Bannockburn was hard-going for horses.
- ✠ At Crécy a small escarpment, giving a vertical drop of 6 feet or so, on the opposite side of the valley to the English position made things difficult for the French cavalry. The French were unable to advance straight towards the enemy position, and were led into a killing ground from which escape was hard.
- ✠ At Poitiers stone walls and hedges created good defences for the English, and created difficulties for the French.

If the terrain is not good, it is possible to transform it. A defensive position can be improved by digging small pits in front of the lines, so as to trip horses as they charge. At Loudoun Hill in 1307 Robert Bruce cunningly narrowed the battlefield by digging trenches. At Castagnaro John Hawkwood had prepared the route in advance for his cavalry to take in their decisive flanking attack.

OPPOSITE *At Crécy in 1346 the English formed up at the top of a slope, on which a windmill stood. Pits dug in front of their archers provided a defence against cavalry. The French were forced by the terrain into a very vulnerable position.*

Morale

You need to be in the right mood to fight, so give your men a good pep talk before battle. Commanders traditionally try to whip up enthusiasm by making speeches, but in the open air, with all the noise of the horses and of men preparing their armour and weapons, it is not easy to hear what is being said. At Poitiers in 1356 the Black Prince is said to have made two speeches, one to the knights and men-at-arms, and the other to the archers. He told the troops that they were descended from true Englishmen:

> *Who, under the lead of my father, and my ancestors, kings of England, found no labour painful, no place invincible, no ground unpassable, no hill however high inaccessible, no tower unscaleable, no army impenetrable, no soldier in arms or host of men formidable.*

The Prince was eloquent, but it is not really necessary to have great skill with words. John Hawkwood had no trouble inspiring his troops, but was said to have been 'more able with hand and industry than with tongue'.

The mood of troops is unpredictable. At Agincourt, the English army was exhausted after the march from Harfleur. Many of the men were suffering from dysentery. Try spending the night in the open, in heavy rain, under orders not to make a sound. You will not feel good in the morning. That is what it was like before the battle, when the English faced an army far larger than their own. Henry V did his best to boost morale, but those who heard him declare that he himself was prepared to die in the conflict cannot have been particularly reassured that victory was theirs for the taking. Yet his resolve was clear, and his example inspirational. Somehow, almost miraculously, the English troops were convinced that they could win. A desperate position was turned into a winning advantage.

OPPOSITE *These knights, shown in an illustration to one of Boccaccio's works, are shown dining in a comfortable, well-equipped tent. Campaigning is not always so luxurious; knights might even find themselves sleeping in the open, holding their horses' reins to prevent them from straying.*

Adagatus dont ie comp
te le cas fut homme igno
ble nez et extraitz du pay

ABOVE Fire is an important weapon in warfare. Campaigning normally sees the ravaging of the countryside and the destruction of villages. Here, common soldiers are shown on the left, torching houses with their flaming brands. The knights look the other way.

BELOW In any war, looting is inevitable. This illustration from a manuscript of Froissart's *Chronicles* shows soldiers staggering under the weight of the plunder that they have taken from an unfortunate town.

OPPOSITE, BELOW The siege of al-Mahdiya by a crusading force under the duke of Bourbon in 1390 was unsuccessful. Food supplies were insufficient, and disease ravaged the army. This illustration shows the town under bombardment from three large siege guns.

ABOVE Bertrand du Guesclin, one of the most successful French commanders of the war with the English, is shown on his deathbed in a tent at the siege of Châteauneuf-de-Randon in 1380. In the foreground there is a large siege bombard on a wheeled carriage, and archers are shown shooting at the defenders of the castle.

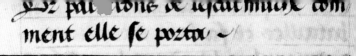

This town is defended by a wooden bastion, from which archers and a crossbowman shoot at their assailants. The besiegers have a large bombard, which shoots stone balls, shown lying beside it. A scaling ladder is being used for the assault, while archers shoot at the garrison.

BELOW The main element in battle is the mêlée, when soldiers engage in fierce hand-to-hand fighting. This illustration shows the fighting at the battle of Poitiers in 1356, at which Edward III of England's son, the Black Prince, captured the French king, John II. Both sides engaged on foot, with common soldiers fighting alongside knights and men-at-arms.

ABOVE The battle of Agincourt. This highly romanticized illustration from
a St Albans chronicle depicts the English victory over the French in 1415.
The English use of archers, shown wearing the red cross of St George, was
a vital element in the battle. The fighting took place on a narrow front,
where horrific piles of slaughtered men built up.

ABOVE This illustration depicts Christ leading a force of crusaders. Nowadays, sadly, the great days of the Crusades are past, but for knights, crusading is still important, and there are many expeditions to join in the Mediterranean and Baltic regions.

RIGHT Ulrich von Liechtenstein wrote an autobiographical book, *The Service of Ladies*, in which he described his adventures when he took part in a large number of tournaments, dressed as Venus. In this illustration he has a magnificently caparisoned horse, and the goddess forms the rather impractical crest on his helmet.

Do not argue

This is easily said. One of the standard explanations for defeat is that there were too many arguments before the battle.

- ✝ At Bannockburn there was a dispute between the earls of Gloucester and Hereford over who had the right to lead the vanguard. Gloucester's subsequent suicidal charge contributed to the English defeat.

- ✝ Before Crécy there was much argument among the French as to whether or not they should attack; it would have made more sense to rest the troops rather than advancing in a headstrong manner.

- ✝ At Nicopolis the crusaders were disunited, with the Franco-Burgundian knights failing to co-operate properly with King Sigismund of Hungary's troops.

It is, however, not only the vanquished whose commanders argue. There was a row at the battle of Auray in 1364, when Hugh Calveley objected to being given command of the rearguard, but nonetheless the Anglo-Breton forces won the battle. Nevertheless, it is safe to assume that if you start arguing over the right tactics, you are likely to be in a bad way once the fighting starts. You should accept the orders you are given with good grace, and not dispute them.

Avoid arranged battles

You may find that your opponents will challenge you to fight a battle on equal terms. Before Poitiers, de Charny suggested that the issue might be settled between one hundred men from each side. You should resist any such suggestions; if you have any sense, you want to ensure that you have the advantage when you fight.

A particularly notable encounter of this sort took place in Brittany in 1351, with the Fight of the Thirty. Jean de Beaumanoir challenged an English captain to a fight between three champions on each side. The

HUGH CALVELEY

Hugh Calveley was a Cheshire man, whose fighting career began in Brittany in the early 1340s, and lasted about 40 years. He was Robert Knollys' brother-in-arms. Calveley captured Bertrand du Guesclin in 1361, and fought at Auray in 1364. He fought alongside his former opponent du Guesclin in Spain in 1366, and was with the Black Prince at Nájera in the next year. Calveley continued to play a distinguished role in the English war with France until the early 1380s; his final campaign was the bishop of Norwich's crusade to Flanders in 1383, and he died in 1394.

English refused, but suggested 20 or 30 on each side, fighting in an agreed location. Rules were settled, with starting signals, breaks for refreshment (a bottle of Anjou wine each), and so forth. The fight was long and hard, and ended in triumph for the French. The English captain and eight of his companions were slain, and the remainder imprisoned. This was a glorious conflict in chivalric terms, and the survivors were always treated with great honour. That does not, however, mean that the challenge was a good idea.

Fighting on horseback

As a knight, the traditional way for you to fight is on horseback. At the start of battle, the cavalry forces look magnificent. The scene when the English drew their cavalry up ready to charge the Scots in 1307 was described by Robert Bruce's biographer, John Barbour:

> *Their bacinets were all burnished bright, gleaming in the sun's light; their spears, their pennons and their shields lit up all the fields with light. Their best, bright-embroidered banners, horse of many hues, coats of armour of diverse colours, and hauberks which were white as flour, made them glitter as though they were like to angels from the kingdom of Heaven.*

The charge is frightening for those standing waiting for the crash of the warhorses as they meet the line of defenders. Again, the life of Robert Bruce provides some impression of what it was like:

If you had come by you would have heard a great crash of the spears that broke, for their enemies attacked fast, galloping on steeds with great arrogance, as if to ride down the earl and all his company.

This is how you should approach fighting in battle on horseback:

✠ When you charge, start slowly, and keep alongside your fellow knights.

✠ Never gallop ahead on your own; only put your spurs to your horse when the enemy is within close range.

✠ Lances are only useful for the initial strike. Many get broken, others cast aside after this.

✠ Once you have penetrated the enemy lines, you are in a mêlée. The best weapon in this hand-to-hand fighting is your sword.

✠ If you can, drive through the enemy lines, turn, and charge them again from the rear.

Fighting on horseback gives an advantage in height, but horses are vulnerable to archers and footsoldiers with pole weapons.

You may find it difficult to remain mounted in the confusion of battle. Pedro IV of Aragon, in his early years, charged into battle in Sardinia. He quickly lost his lance and was unhorsed, but continued to fight on foot. He was struck no fewer than 19 blows, but once he got hold of his sword, which he called *Villardelle*, the enemy began to fall back in disarray.

Fighting on horseback can sometimes work well. The French cavalry triumphed at Cassel in 1328, and again at Roosebeke in 1382, when French and Burgundian cavalry defeated the townspeople of Ghent. At Poitiers it was the cavalry under the Gascon Captal de Buch who dealt the final hammer blow to the French. There are, however, major potential problems if you do choose to fight in battle in this way.

The failure of the mounted knight

Worryingly for knights, recent history shows that you are more likely to face defeat if you try to fight on horseback:

✝ The battle of Courtrai in 1302 saw the Flemish townspeople, fighting on foot, defeat the flower of French chivalry.

✝ At Bannockburn in 1314 the English cavalry were cut down by Scottish spearmen.

✝ Swiss troops fighting on foot, with long halberds, were successful against knightly cavalry at Morgarten in 1315.

✝ The Swiss infantry were successful against aristocratic cavalry at Laupen in 1339.

✝ The English broke the French cavalry in spectacular fashion at Crécy; archery was one key to their success, but in the mêlée it was the dismounted English knights and men-at-arms who won the battle.

✝ At Nájera in 1367 the Black Prince's troops were successful against the cavalry of Henry of Trastamara, the claimant to the Castilian throne.

This imaginative picture of the battle of Neville's Cross in 1346, from a manuscript of Froissart's Chronicles, *shows mounted knights in the foreground, fighting with lances and swords.*

✝ At Aljubarrota in 1385 English dismounted forces, including archers, assisted the Portuguese in their defeat of the Franco-Castilian army.

✝ At Sempach in 1386 the Swiss infantry defeated the Austrian cavalry.

The crusading battle of Nicopolis in 1396 was the final demonstration of the failure of the mounted knight. There, Boucicaut fought with exceptional bravery. He spurred his great charger, his sword in his hand, and rode through the Turkish ranks, turning his horse to assist his companions. Inevitably, he was captured. His biographer described the odds, 20 Saracens against one Christian (believe that if you want). He considered that the defeat was the fault of the Hungarian troops, not of the noble French knights who displayed such courage and valour, but the fact remains that the knights were a failure. Turkish archers were important in Sultan Bāyazîd's triumph; by aiming at the horses they destroyed half of the duke of Burgundy's cavalry.

Be ready to fight on foot

Since there are such dangers in fighting on horseback, think again about it. The most effective tactic is for you to stand close-packed with your colleagues, knights, squires and men-at-arms, and face the enemy on foot. This tactic was first developed by the English.

✝ The English government gave instructions in 1327 that the knights and men-at-arms were not to bring their great warhorses on campaign against the Scots. They were drawn up on foot for battle, though on this occasion the Scots withdrew and did not fight.

✝ In 1332 the method worked brilliantly, when a small English force dismounted to face the Scots at Dupplin Moor. By selecting a perfect defensive position the English nullified the advantage that the Scots had in numbers, and cut them down as they advanced on the English line. The trick was repeated in 1333 at Halidon Hill.

✝ In 1346 similar tactics were used at Crécy, with the English employing dismounted knights and men-at-arms flanked by archers.

OPPOSITE *The English longbow is usually 6 feet or more in length, and requires great strength and much practice to shoot. These archers, shown in a manuscript of about 1340, carry quivers, each containing two dozen arrows.*

Do not advance on foot

It is advisable to fight on foot, but do not tire yourself out by marching far. At Poitiers, the French, on the advice of the Scot William Douglas, dismounted the bulk of their cavalry. They did not, however, fight from a defensive position, but advanced on the English lines. This meant that they were exhausted by the time they were able to engage their enemy, and in no fit state to face a gruelling mêlée.

Agincourt provides another example; the French were worn out by the time they reached the English position. It is no fun advancing on foot through a muddy field, being shot at by English archers, particularly if you are weighed down by armour. You will be quite out of breath even before you start fighting. So, whatever you do, don't advance if you are on foot. The whole idea of dismounting to fight is that your army should establish a strong defensive position, and wait to be attacked.

Watch out for archers

One of the main reasons for English success in battle has been the use of longbowmen. Their bow is a simple, but deadly, weapon. A trained man can shoot off a dozen arrows in a minute, and they are effective over a range of at least 200 yards. The sight of a cloud of arrows, with the hissing sound

that they make as they fall towards you, is terrifying. The horses are particularly affected, and will buck and turn as they are maddened by the stinging missiles. These archers proved their worth at Crécy and at Poitiers.

The role of English archers has been influential on more distant battlefields. At Aljubarrota the archers in the Anglo-Portuguese army 'shot so vigorously and quick that the horses were larded, as it were, with arrows, and fell one upon the other.' Archers under John Hawkwood were important in his victory at Castagnaro in 1387. Turkish archers are also to be feared. The Turks do not draw their bows back quite as far as the English, just to the moustache, not the ear. Their bows, however, are strong, and their arrows frightening.

There are ways of dealing with archers; at the battle of Auray in 1364 the English bowmen were countered by the French knights and men-at-arms, who were well-armoured and used their shields to good effect. They were in such close order that 'one could scarcely throw an apple among them, without it falling on a helmet or lance.'

How to fight in the mêlée

It is hard to describe what happens in the midst of battle. The noise is unbearable, with horses neighing, men shouting and swords clashing. Barbour's *The Bruce* puts it well:

> *There was such a din of blows, such as weapons landing on armour, such a great breaking of spears, such pressure and such pushing, such snarling and groaning, so much noise as they struck the others, and shouted rallying cries on both sides, giving and receiving great wounds, that it was horrible to hear.*

Keep close to your companions; getting isolated is very dangerous. Make sure you are aware of what is happening around you, and fight as best you can. It probably will not last that long; most battles go on for no more than a few hours. If you are lucky, there will be a half-time break; at the battle of Neville's Cross in 1346 both sides laid down their weapons at least once, so as to get their breath.

Be very careful not to get caught in the middle. The press of men can become too great, as those behind push forward, but those in front cannot move. This was the case above all at Dupplin Moor in 1332 and at Agincourt in 1415. The result is horrendous; as men are forced up to the front line, they climb over their comrades. Those beneath are suffocated, and piles of dead and dying men are built up. An eye-witness describes Agincourt:

> *Such a great heap grew of the slain and of those lying crushed in between that our men climbed up those heaps, which had risen above a man's height, and butchered their enemies down below with swords, axes and other weapons.*

Never think that the fighting in battle is going to be a glorious experience, a splendid opportunity to demonstrate your knightly skills. It is going

The mêlée at Aljubarrota in 1385 was fierce. Here, men fight hand-to-hand, as well as with bow and lance.

OF BATTLES

Bannockburn, with two days of fighting, was the longest battle to take place in the 14th century.

✝

At Crécy Edward III did not get involved in the fighting directly, but stayed by a windmill from where he could observe the battle.

✝

Muslim armies make the most noise before battle, with drums, trumpets, cymbals and fifes.

Remarkably, the English knight Maurice Berkeley succeeded in getting himself captured by the French, during the English victory at Poitiers.

✝

At the battle of Tannenberg the Polish king, fearing what would happen if his men got drunk, ordered the destruction of the wine-barrels found in the German baggage train.

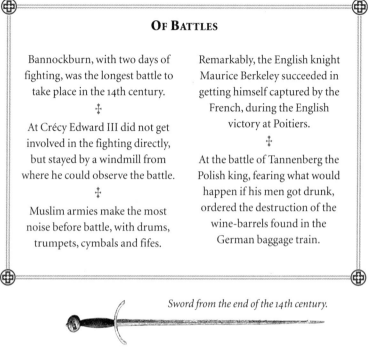

Sword from the end of the 14th century.

to be noisy, crowded and utterly terrifying. The mêlée at Tannenberg in 1410, described by the chronicler Jan Dlugosz, provides an example:

> *Breaking spears and armour hitting against each other produced such a great clatter and bang, and the clang of swords resounded so loudly, as if some huge rock had collapsed, that even those who were several miles away could hear it. Then knight attacked knight, armour crushed under the pressure of armour, and swords hit faces. And when the ranks closed, it was impossible to tell the coward from the brave, the bold from the slow, because all of them were pressed together, as if in some tangle.*

This sort of fighting can offer opportunities for heroism. James Audley vowed to be in the front line in any battle involving Edward III or his son, and carried this out at Poitiers in 1356, as Froissart described:

He was severely wounded in the body, head and face; and as long as
his strength and breath permitted him, he maintained the fight, and
advanced forward; he continued to do so until he was covered with
blood; then, towards the close of the engagement, his four squires who
were his bodyguard, took him, and led him out of the engagement,
very weak and wounded.

Audley survived, and was praised by the Black Prince as the bravest knight in the battle. His example, however, would be dangerous to follow.

Do not try to be a hero

Of course knights should be valorous and brave, but don't take this to excesses in the way that some have done. One man cannot defeat an army.

✠ On the first day at the battle of Bannockburn William Deyncourt, 'bold of heart and hand', galloped all alone into the lines of Scottish footsoldiers. He was brought down and killed, without thought of the ransom he would have been worth.

✠ On the second day at Bannockburn the young earl of Gloucester charged single-handed into the Scottish lines; the knights of his retinue had more sense than to follow him. He was duly slain.

✠ At the end of the battle of Bannockburn, Giles of Argentein could not bear to leave the battlefield in defeat, but committed himself to one last suicidal charge. 'Assuredly I never yet fled, and I choose to stay here and die, rather than live in shame by flight.' His reputation survived, but he did not.

✠ On the Nájera campaign in 1367 William Felton 'boldly and bravely threw himself on horseback into the enemy like a madman'. He killed a Spaniard with his lance, drew his sword and dealt with another, but then his horse was slain under him, and he was himself killed.

Such chivalrous feats may be magnificent, but they are not war.

Do not underestimate your foe

When Boucicaut fought his first battle, at Roosebeke in 1382, he was just 16. He found himself engaging a large Flemish man-at-arms. The Fleming knocked Boucicaut's axe from his hand, saying 'Go and suck, go, child. Now I can see that the French have no men, since their children fight in battles.' Boucicaut, very upset at the loss of his axe, promptly drew his dagger, and stabbed the man under his armpit, saying, as he killed him, 'Do the children in your country play games like these?'

In practice, you probably won't find yourself faced by many children in battle, but watch out for the unexpected. It is common in the later stages of a battle for the infantry to enter the mêlée to do their worst. That apparently insignificant footsoldier, lacking armour and proper equipment, may have a dagger or knife with which to give you a nasty injury.

You may think, if you are on crusade, that you are superior to your foes, because God is on your side. This is a dangerous view, as the events at Nicopolis showed. If you are facing Turks, they are just as confident as you are that God is supporting them, and if you have Lithuanians against you, they believe that there is a whole host of gods backing their cause.

Gunpowder weapons

Do not worry about these; they are hopeless on the battlefield, and surely will remain so. The English had some guns at the battle of Crécy. They made a big noise, and produced a lot of smoke, but achieved little. One problem is that it takes far too long to load a gun. The Italians have tried to do something about this, and developed a weapon in the form of a cart with no fewer than 12 dozen guns mounted on it, so as to deliver a fearful volley. The Veronese tried this out at Castagnaro in 1387; it did not work.

Forget your vows

It is very likely that you have made vows to perform valiant deeds. It is particularly dangerous if these relate to battle, as James Audley found out. It is said, for example, that the 89 knights of the Company of the Star who died in Brittany at the battle of Mauron in 1352 did so because they had sworn never to flee from the battlefield. It is very possible that the determination of the blind king of Bohemia, John of Luxembourg, to enter the fray at Crécy was because of a vow that he had made. It will be possible for you to obtain absolution from your vows; it is not worth putting yourself in unnecessary danger because of a foolish promise you made when you were probably drunk.

What happens if you lose?

Men get wounded and killed in battles, and there is no easy way to keep yourself safe. There are no reliable counts, but large numbers of fatalities are often reported. The chronicler Jean le Bel was exaggerating when he claimed that at Crécy the total of dead came to nine princes and about 12,000 knights, with 15,000 or 16,000 common soldiers, but it is clear that the death toll was horrendous.

If you find yourself on the wrong side in a rout, remember that is when most casualties occur. Rivers are a particular hazard, for they often block escape routes; when people cannot cross them, they drown. The scene after Bannockburn, described in Barbour's life of Robert Bruce, was truly horrific:

> Truth to tell, they were so terrified, and they fled in fear so fast, that a very great part of them fled to the River Forth and there most of them were drowned; Bannockburn between its banks was so filled with men and horses that men could then pass dry-foot over it on drowned horses and men.

It is said that after the battle of Nájera in Spain in 1367, many of the defeated chose to jump in the river and drown, rather than be slaughtered. If you do not fancy a watery grave, instead of fleeing when defeat threatens, the best thing to do is to find an enemy knight and surrender to him. You will have to pay your captor a ransom, but that's a small price to pay for your life. If that does not appeal to you, get rid of your armour and hide; you might be able to make your escape eventually. What you must not do is panic and flee; that is a sure way to get yourself killed.

Ransoms & Booty

This Sir Eustace ... won great wealth for himself through ransoms, through sale of towns and castles, and also through redemption of estates and houses and the safe-conducts he provided.

FROISSART'S *CHRONICLES*, 1358

‡   ‡   ‡

ou will probably not have learned much in your training about how to make money. The chivalric values include liberality, but not entrepreneurial skills or business acumen. Geoffroi de Charny has some advice in his book, but you will not find it helpful if you want to make your fortune in war. He cautions you against placing too much emphasis on winning booty and making profits, for these may not last in the way that honour does. He counsels you against too much display and outward show, and points out that if you spend too much, you will have to abandon your military exploits. The implication is that you should match your income against your costs. The best knight, for de Charny, is one who takes dangerous risks and accepts physical hardship so as to perform great deeds of arms, with no expectation of reward other than personal honour.

De Charny may not have recognized this, but war is big business. There is money to be made, though you need to assess the risks. It is important to note that the value of investments can go down as well as up, so you may get back less than you put in. You can do very well out of ransoms, and levying protection money on villages and towns provides an easy way to earn substantial sums. There is booty there for the taking. If you are sensible, you can make a fortune, but not many do.

Ransoms

When you take someone prisoner, you can hold them to ransom. This has distinct advantages. It means that you can make significant profits; it also means that it makes little sense to kill your enemies, so battles become a bit less dangerous. Before the battle of Auray in 1364, the English commander, John Chandos, was considering whether to negotiate rather than to fight, but a group of knights and squires begged him to engage in battle. They were poor, they said, and they hoped to recover their fortunes in the fight.

You have got to be careful; there are occasions when ransoms are not available. These are best avoided, because if you are captured, you may be killed, and if you are victorious, there is no money to be made. The Flemings at Courtrai in 1302 took no ransoms; there was a massive death toll among the French as a result. At the battle of Crécy both kings, Philip VI and Edward III, gave orders that this was *guerre à l'outrance*, war to the uttermost, and no quarter was to be given. Neither king wished to see his

Payment of a ransom. Jean de Beaumanoir, a Breton hero, handing over 100,000 francs in 1387 to the duke of Brittany's representatives, to obtain the release of Olivier de Clisson, constable of France.

men distracted from the business of fighting by that of negotiating surrenders and ransoms. As a result, the English took far fewer prisoners for ransom than would be expected from a major victory. Watch out in particular for the Swiss. They are not interested in money (and surely never will be), and do not as a rule ransom their prisoners. At Sempach in 1386 the duke of Austria and a large number of his knights were slain.

Taking a prisoner

You need to be careful not to injure your opponent too badly in the heat of battle, for a dead prisoner is worth nothing. When, in the mid-1360s, John Amory was taken by Guichard d'Albigon, he was seriously wounded. Guichard did his best to save him, taking him to a nearby town, but unfortunately Amory bled to death, and a good potential ransom was lost.

Another problem is that you may have trouble from the common soldiers in the army, who like nothing more than slaughtering knights; when Henry de Quenillart captured Eustace d'Auberchicourt in 1359, he had great difficulty protecting him, as the troops were keen to kill him in revenge for his earlier deeds.

LEFT A list drawn up in November 1410 of the Teutonic Knights captured at the battle of Tannenberg. Most of the knights were killed in the battle, and massive ransoms were demanded for the release of those who were taken prisoner.

OPPOSITE A knight captured in battle is led off into captivity.

Once you have found a prisoner, you need to make sure that he or she is yours alone. At Poitiers the count of Dammartin initially surrendered to a squire, handing him his bacinet. Then a Gascon appeared, threateningly, and the count gave him a shield as a sign of capture, and a third would-be captor obtained an oath from the count. In the end, the count became the prisoner of the earl of Salisbury.

There can be disasters. At Agincourt, Henry V was alarmed by the possibility of a French counter-attack, and so ordered the killing of the prisoners. That may have been understandable as an act of military logic, but it was financial folly to lose the chance of securing all those ransoms.

How large should a ransom be?

You will hear some very large sums bandied about:

✝ The counts of Vendôme, Tancarville and Eu, taken at Poitiers in 1356, had ransoms set at 30,000 florins each.

✝ According to Froissart, the ransoms agreed after the battle of Launac, near Toulouse, in 1362 totalled 1,000,000 francs, and documents show that this was not much of an exaggeration.

Avoid the temptation to think in such terms. Consider whether it likely that your prisoner can raise the money.

✝ John Hawkwood captured a Sienese commander in 1366, and asked for 10,000 florins as ransom, but in the end he had to be content with just 500.

EXCHANGE RATES

Exchange rates fluctuate considerably, but as a general rule, a franc, a *mouton d'or*, an écu, a florin, a ducat and the Castilian *dobla*, all gold coins, are fairly similar in value, at around 3s. sterling. Silver currency is expressed in pounds, which are units of account rather than coins. Twelve pennies make a shilling, and 20 shillings a pound. There are about 6 or 7 French pounds, or *livres tournois*, to an English pound sterling. Therefore one of the gold coins is worth roughly one *livre*, but there are about 6 or 7 of them to a pound sterling.

✠ A huge ransom of 700,000 écus was set for Charles of Blois, captured by the English in 1347, but no more than 50,000 écus were actually received by Edward III.

✠ Even the realistic ransom of two tuns of wine, agreed when Renaud le Vicomte was captured in 1358, caused problems when the wine was stolen and Renaud could not pay up.

Remember that if you take a really important prisoner, it won't be up to you to determine the ransom. When John of Coupland captured the king of Scots at Neville's Cross in 1346, after spotting him hiding under a bridge, John had to hand him over to the crown. He obtained his reward in the form of a grant of £500 a year for life. That was only a tiny fraction of the total ransom of £66,666, but John could hardly have hoped for more.

Selling the ransom

If you are an ordinary knight, you should not try to hold an important prisoner for long, and attempt to negotiate payment of his ransom yourself. You should get rid of your prisoner as fast as possible. There is a trade in ransoms. You may not obtain the highest possible price if you sell your prisoner on, but at least you will have made some money, and you will save yourself a great deal of bother.

✝ Walter Mauny captured Guy de Rickenburg in 1337, and a ransom of £11,000 was agreed. Mauny then handed his prisoner over to Edward III in return for £8,000. Guy, however, agreed to change sides, and so no ransom was paid. Considering this, Mauny did rather well out of the situation.

✝ Two knights, William Berland and Thomas Cheyne, took Bertrand du Guesclin prisoner at Nájera; they sold their rights in him to the Black Prince for £3,000 each. The ransom was then set at 100,000 gold *doblas*. The two knights may have felt that they had lost out, but they would not have been in a position to negotiate an agreement in the way that the prince could do.

Ransom disputes

If you don't sell your prisoner on, you will almost certainly face many difficulties. The two squires who captured the count of Denia at Nájera in 1367 did not take the same sensible attitude as the knights who captured du Guesclin. Instead, they asked for a huge ransom of 150,000 *doblas*. The count was exchanged for his son, but found it impossible to raise the money. The English government was keen to help, for diplomatic reasons, but the squires were adamant. They wanted their money. The outcome was that they were imprisoned in the Tower, and escaped, to take sanctuary in Westminster Abbey. The constable of the Tower pursued them there, and one of them was killed. Legal disputes over the money dragged on and on for many years.

How can you pay a ransom?

Even great soldiers get taken prisoner. Bertrand du Guesclin was certainly captured twice, and probably more often than that. Boucicaut was a prisoner twice, once after the battle of Nicopolis, and again after Agincourt. So, you may well get captured, and have a ransom to pay. If you are important enough, you may receive assistance from many quarters.

✠ Du Guesclin was captured by John Chandos at Auray in 1364, and was taken again by the Black Prince's forces at Nájera. His ransom costs were largely met by Charles V of France, Henry of Trastamara and the Pope.

✠ After Boucicaut was captured by the Turks at Nicopolis, there were complex negotiations for freeing him and the other prisoners. The initial suggestion of a million florins for all those captured was reduced to 200,000 florins, and Venetian bankers played an important role in transferring the money, which was mostly collected in Burgundy and France. Boucicaut himself had to raise 10,000 francs, but at least he did not have to pay the full amount needed for his release.

If you are lucky, your followers might come to your rescue. Eustace d'Auberchicourt was captured by the French in 1359, and a ransom of 22,000 *livres* was demanded. He was fortunate, for the troops he had been commanding clubbed together to raise the money. Even though he had a rich wife, it would not have been possible for him to raise such a sum out of his normal income.

Arrangements for payment can get very complicated. The ransom due to the earl of Salisbury for the count of Dammartin, taken at Poitiers in 1356, was set at 12,000 florins. This may not seem excessive in comparison with some ransom figures, but Dammartin could not raise the cash. It was agreed instead that an estate in Somerset, which belonged to another French noble, Robert de Fiennes, should be transferred to the earl. In return, Dammartin would transfer property in France to Fiennes. This led to complex litigation about the value of the various lands, and it was not until 1370, long after the count's release, that the issues were settled.

Protection money

If you read Geoffroi de Charny's book about chivalry, you will find that he condemns those who rob, steal and take booty and prisoners without proper justification. In reality, there are renowned knights, such as Eustace d'Auberchicourt, who have done very well for themselves by exploiting the resources of the land. Even the virtuous Boucicaut received 15,000 ducats a month from towns in Lombardy in exchange for a truce.

If you are occupying part of a country, you can take advantage of your position by levying protection money on the local peasantry. These sums are known as *appatis*. You can suggest to those who pay that you are offering them some form of protection in return, or you can simply take their money. If they are reluctant to pay up, imprison them, burn their property, set your men on their women, and they will soon come to terms. This may not sound very chivalrous, but there is no need to be scrupulous when dealing with peasants.

In Italy there are big profits to be made from extortion. In 1364 the Company of the Star, under Haneken Bongard and Albert Sterz, obtained 38,650 florins from Siena, and 11 years later John Hawkwood was paid 30,500 florins by the same city. A letter he and a German associate wrote to the authorities in Siena in 1374 explained:

If it pleases your lordships to spend a certain amount of money on this company, as customarily ought to be spent on men-at-arms, we will abstain from damage and, so far as we can, we will keep your territory free from harm: but if not, we will allow pillagers from that company to do whatever they wish.

The White Company in Italy had its specialized *guastatori*, whose expertise was in laying the land and its settlements waste. It was well worth paying out to avoid their attentions. One calculation is that the money paid to the mercenaries by the city of Siena between 1342 and 1399 would have been sufficient to enable them to buy the cities of Avignon, Montpellier and Lucca.

Booty

If you are successful in war, there is booty to be won, sometimes on a massive scale. The English did very well for themselves in some their invasions of France. After the town of Caen was sacked in 1346, it was said that there was not a matron in England who was not decked with finery taken

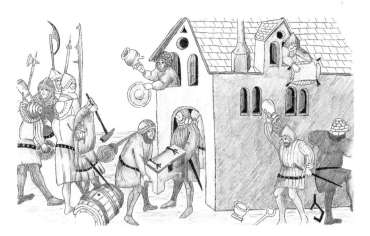

Soldiers looting a house. Pillaging like this is a regular part of warfare. There are rules about the way in which the booty should be divided up. A commander can normally claim at least a third.

there. There is much to be found in cellars, storehouses and barns; your men will become skilled at hunting out treasure from all sorts of hiding places. Hopefully they will be reliable and will hand over your share.

A note of goods taken from Robert Knollys in 1354, when he was temporarily in disgrace, suggests the kind of things you may expect to find. The list includes:

> 1 silver basin and ewer,
> total weight 7 lbs.
> 4 silver chargers.
> 18 silver saucers.
>
> 2 goatskins.
> 2 new pairs of boots.

Sharing the gains

Remember that you don't get to keep all that you may win. There are conventions for dividing up the spoils; it is normal for a commander to claim a third, or even a half, of your gains. In the case of ransoms, you may get much less than that if the sum involved is large. An indenture between the duke of York and Thomas Gerberge in 1388 set out the terms:

*The lord will have the third part of all gains of war that Sir Thomas
shall make with his own hands, and the third part of the thirds of his
retinue, and if it happens that the said Thomas or any of his retinue
take a captain or peer of the realm, a castle or fortress from our
enemies, the said lord duke shall give reasonable satisfaction to he
who had made the capture as can be well agreed between them.*

You may be able to get away without declaring everything that you have
taken in the course of a campaign, but in any calculations you make,
remember that your gains are, in effect, subject to heavy taxation.

Profit and loss

'I have at times been so miserably poor that I had not a horse to mount, at
other times rich enough, just as good fortune befell me,' remarked the
Bascot de Mauléon to Froissart, when the two men met in the Hotel de la
Lune at Orthez in 1388. You should not be too convinced by the success
stories that you hear; not everyone can be a winner. There is no consistent
pattern, but if you are on the winning side, you are likely to do well. It is not
just a matter of obtaining ransoms and plunder; you also need to know
what to do with your gains; you must be a businessman as well as a warrior.
Putting your money into property is a good idea; gold, silver and jewels can
be squandered all too easily. You should also keep proper accounts, which
will help you to meet any claims made against you.

Robert Knollys provides an example to follow. He bore a banner in
1358, which arrogantly declared that he was worth 100,000 *moutons d'or*,
and he certainly made a lot in the wars between England and France.
Though he was known as a generous captain, he was careful with his
money, and used some of his gains to buy up property in Norfolk. He
developed interests in trade and finance, even lending money to the crown.
His close associate Hugh Calveley appears to have done less well; promises
of castles in Spain, and of substantial pensions, came to nothing.

John Hawkwood had an income by 1377 that was greater than that of
the city of Lucca, but by 1393 he was complaining that his funds were inade-
quate to meet the needs of his family. He sent some money back to

THE BASCOT DE MAULÉON

Froissart included in his chronicle a long account of the life of this Gascon soldier of fortune. The Bascot de Mauléon fought at Poitiers, went on crusade in the Baltic, and joined in the slaughter of the rebellious peasants at Meaux. He became a mercenary captain, was at the battle of Brignais in 1362, and fought with Hugh Calveley at Auray in 1364. He went with Calveley to Spain, and then returned to fight in Gascony. You may think that Froissart has made all this up, but no, the Bascot was not a figment of the chronicler's imagination.

England, and was able to buy a few manors in Essex, and Leadenhall in London, but most of the wealth that he accumulated in Italy seems to have evaporated. His is a cautionary tale of someone who made a lot of money, but who also spent a great deal, despite the efforts of his business-like wife.

Boucicaut is the example you should absolutely not follow. He may be held up as an example of a chivalric hero in the classic mould, but in financial management he leaves a great deal to be desired.

✝ His crusading enterprises were costly.

✝ He made no money from his time as governor of Genoa, and by the end of it he was in a desperate financial plight. He had to borrow from Italian bankers, and had to pawn or sell his own treasure of jewels and plate. A coronet belonging to his wife, her jewelry, and even a golden statue of the Virgin Mary had to go.

✝ When he arrived back in France, his attempts to recover some of his costs from the crown were hampered by his lack of business-like methods, for he could not produce the requisite receipts and documentation to show what he had spent. He finally received about half of what he was owed.

✝ The final disaster is that he cannot pay the ransom demanded after his capture at Agincourt.

The risks

It would be easy to claim in a business plan that you will make a lot of money as a knight. Ransoms, booty and protection money can all go down as large potential profits. The risks, however, are considerable. You may well find that promised wages are not forthcoming; that you have to pay your own ransom; that lands you have won cost more to defend than they produce in revenue; that at least a third of your gains has to be paid to your lord. Think hard about it; going to war is a high-risk strategy if you are more concerned about making money than winning fame and glory.

RIGHT *Seal of Guy de Dampierre, count of Flanders. He was captured by the count of Hainault, and ransomed in 1256. In 1296 he had to pay King Philip IV of France to release him from captivity. He was captured again in 1300, and died, a prisoner of the French, in 1304.*

LEFT *A French écu of 1305.*

OF GAINS OF WAR

It is said that when Raoul of Tancarville, who was taken prisoner by the English in 1347, returned to France he praised his captors so much that the French king had him executed.

✝

Gifts presented to John Hawkwood, Albert Stertz and Haneken Bongard by the city of Siena included sweets.

The constable of England is entitled to all cattle without horns, pigs and unshod horses as booty, and is supposed to receive 4d. a week from all whores and merchants following the army.

✝

The capture of Alexandria by the crusaders in 1365 yielded more than 70 shiploads of booty.

Piety & Memory

*If a knight die in war ordained by the church, as in the case of
war against the unbelievers or of the faith, and is not otherwise
in mortal sin, his soul goes straight to paradise.*

HONORÉ BOUVET, *THE TREE OF BATTLES,* 1387

✣   ✣   ✣

ou don't want to go to hell. If you end up there, you will find
yourself wearing armour that you cannot take off, for it will be
nailed onto you. You will be forced to take lots of baths, and to
make matters worse, the water will be sulphurous and foul.
Nor will you have amorous young women to embrace when you get out;
instead, lustful toads will force themselves on you. There are steps you can
take to avoid this fate.

Pious donations

It is too much to hope that you will have been consistently good and virtuous throughout your knightly career. You will probably regret, for example,
the way in which you have assisted in the destruction of churches and
monasteries in the course of your campaigns. You may have done your best
to hear mass; perhaps you had papal permission to have a portable altar,
and it is likely that you will have given alms when the opportunity arose.
You need, however, to do more. A good way to avoid a painful and unpleasant afterlife is to ensure that you have lots of masses said for you after your
death. You could follow the example of Jean de Grailly, the Captal de Buch.
His will specified that 50,000 masses were to be said for him in the year
following his death. He gave 1,000 écus to the house of the Franciscans at
Bordeaux, and in all his various pious donations totalled 40,000 écus.

There are many examples of pious donations. Boucicaut gave to the chapter of St Martin of Tours, and in 1406 founded a hospital at Sainte-Catherine-de-Fierbois. Robert Knollys founded a college of clergy at Pontefract, probably because his wife came from there. He also put funds towards the rebuilding of Rochester Bridge. Walter Mauny gave to the London Charterhouse. Ralph, Lord Basset of Drayton gave £250 to the priory of Canwell, so that there could be five more monks there; he also arranged for the foundation of four chantries. In Italy in 1364 the German mercenary Albert Bylandt built the convent of San Antonio in Vicenza, where he was buried with his wife Aquilia.

Even if you do not make such expensive arrangements, you need to ensure that your will provides for a good funeral, and a proper number of

A painted alabaster carving from the tomb of Ferdinand Antequera,
king of Aragon, showing part of his funeral procession.

prayers to be said for you. In his will of 1385, John Devereux set out his wishes, which included paying the poor to pray for him:

> *My body is to be buried in the church of the Grey Friars in London, and I will that six tapers in the form of a cross be placed upon my hearse, and that six men clothed in white bear six torches, and that each of them receive 40d. for his pains; also to every poor man at my burial one penny to pray for my soul, and for all Christian souls; to the Grey Friars for my burial there 40 marks, and I will that as soon as possible after my death one thousand masses be said for my soul, and for the souls of my father and mother.*

Bertrand du Guesclin, in his will, arranged for a mass to be said every day for him in the Breton town of Dinan, and for pilgrims to go on his behalf to two shrines in Brittany. You will find that religious houses are eager to receive your money; in Lucca in Italy in 1346 there was an unseemly dispute between two churches over which of them should say masses for the German Johann von Geispolzheim.

Your tomb

You will almost certainly be much more concerned about having a large number of masses said for your soul, than you will be about the quality of your tomb. Nevertheless, a good tomb will help to ensure that you are remembered and honoured by future generations. A relatively cheap option is to have a memorial brass; these are a very popular form of monument, especially in England. There are workshops in London that specialize in making them, and you can be sure that you will be shown smartly attired in the very latest style of armour. One problem is that brasses tend to be rather stylized; one knight looks very much like another. A full-sized effigy is a far grander way of doing things; you might think of having one in alabaster, painted to look lifelike. This is what Walter Mauny wanted:

> *I will that a tomb of alabaster, with my image as a knight, and my arms thereon, shall be made for me, like that of Sir John Beauchamp, in St Paul's, in London.*

A canopied tomb looks particularly good, if you and your family can afford it. If you are really fortunate, someone else may want to pay. The Florentines were keen to have a grand tomb for John Hawkwood, but Richard II foiled their plan when he demanded that the body should be brought back to England. The Florentines had to settle instead for a splendid fresco in the cathedral to commemorate Hawkwood.

OPPOSITE *Two English brasses, showing Matthew de Swetenham, and John de Creke.*

RIGHT *Two German tombstones, one of Gunther von Schwarzburg, who was elected as German king in 1349 and died in the same year, and the other of Albert von Hohenlohe.*

Resurrection

You ought to try to make sure that you are buried all in one piece. In 1299 Pope Boniface VIII prohibited the burying of different body parts in different places, but it was difficult to enforce this, and 50 years later Clement V allowed the practice once again. There are all sorts of theological difficulties involved if a body is not whole. The theologian Thomas of Chobham put one of the problems like this:

> *Certain people object that if Christ was resurrected in glory and His whole body was glorified, how is it that the Church claims that Christ's foreskin, cut off at the time of his circumcision, still remains on earth?*

There are cases of notable warriors being buried in separate bits. Remember Robert Bruce, whose heart was taken off to Spain on crusade by James Douglas. Douglas was killed fighting, but fortunately Bruce's heart was found on the battlefield and taken back to Scotland. However, it was buried at Melrose Abbey, not with the rest of Bruce's body at Dunfermline. It will surely cause a lot of unnecessary work when it comes to the Resurrection if you have to be reassembled from a number of locations, and there is even a danger that you may end up incomplete.

Memoirs

One way in which you can ensure that your knightly deeds will be remembered by posterity is to have a book written about you. If you are fortunate enough to meet Jean Froissart, he might include stories about you in his chronicles. Alternatively, you could follow the example of Pedro IV of Aragon and write an autobiography, though it is unlikely that you will have the time for this. Ulrich von Liechtenstein also wrote up part of his own career, though it is hard to know how seriously to take his adventures as a tournament hero dressed as a woman.

The French are particularly keen on having very long books to glorify their careers. Boucicaut's *Life* was written during his lifetime, primarily in order to justify his actions as governor of Genoa, but also to set out all his

SOME FINAL TIPS

Train hard. Climbing up the reverse side of ladders is a good form of exercise.

✝

Get knighted on the battlefield; it's much simpler that way.

✝

Buy your armour in Milan.

✝

Keep your legs straight when you ride.

✝

Keep your eye on the target, not on the tip of your lance.

✝

Do not make unnecessary or dangerous vows.

✝

Find a sensible girl to adore.

Do not crusade against the Mamluks or the Turks.

✝

Get off your horse to fight battles.

✝

If you want a souvenir from your travels, think about bringing back a leopard.

✝

Keep away from guns; they may explode in your face.

✝

Have as little to do with peasants as possible.

✝

Do not dress up in flammable fancy dress.

✝

Do not be too greedy in setting ransom demands.

achievements up to 1409. Bertrand du Guesclin's life is celebrated by an enormous work in bad verse by Jean Cuvelier. There are also plans for a large book by Jean Cabaret d'Orville on Louis de Bourbon. For some reason the English have not gone in for long works of this sort; all that they can offer is a brief verse life of the Black Prince by the Chandos Herald. Nor do the Germans or Italians indulge in lengthy biographies.

If you do well, being a knight can offer you magnificent possibilities for fame and fortune. It is even possible, if you are really successful, that your deeds may be celebrated in books written in the distant future, perhaps even in the 21st century.

Sir John Chandos at the head of his troops (and shortly before he was killed after tripping over his surcoat).

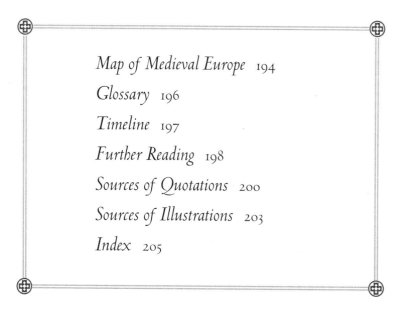

Map of Medieval Europe 194

Glossary 196

Timeline 197

Further Reading 198

Sources of Quotations 200

Sources of Illustrations 203

Index 205

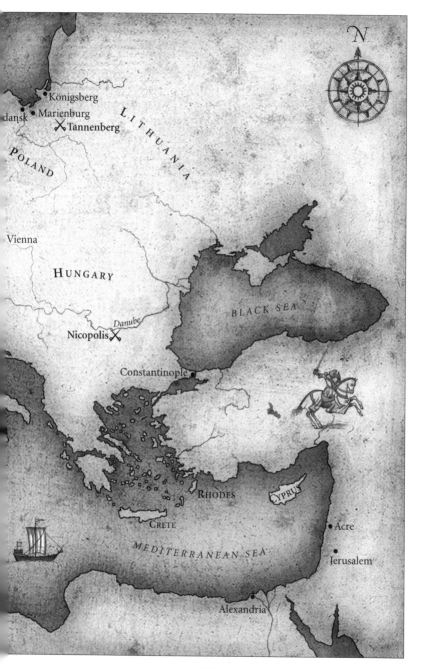

Königsberg

dansk Marienburg

POLAND

✕Tannenberg

LITHUANIA

Vienna

HUNGARY

BLACK SEA

Danube

Nicopolis✕

Constantinople

RHODES

CYPRUS

CRETE

Acre

MEDITERRANEAN SEA

Jerusalem

Alexandria

Glossary

almogàver Spanish infantry soldier

appatis protection money levied on towns and villages

bacinet pointed helmet, often with a vizor

banneret military rank, superior to a knight

barbuta unit in an Italian army consisting of a knight and page

bath receptacle used, probably rarely, for washing by immersion

béhourd form of tournament, often providing training for young men

billeting provision of lodging for troops

Black Prince Edward, Prince of Wales, son of King Edward III of England

booty goods captured in war

brother-in-arms partner in war, with whom profits and losses were shared

campaign major military expedition

chevauchée mounted raid

charger a top-quality warhorse

coat of arms heraldic symbol or design, often on a shield, designating a particular family

coronal blunt end piece of a tournament lance

crusade religious war, conducted under papal authorization

damsel young lady

destrier a top-quality warhorse

feudal service military service owed in return for land

florin coin, originally from Florence, worth about three English shillings

garrison body of troops defending a castle or town

guastatori men used in Italian armies for ravaging and destroying

garter article of clothing, puzzlingly used by Edward III as the symbol of his order of knighthood

harbinger man who goes in advance of the army to arrange accommodation

hackney Riding horse of no great value

heraldry the art of devising and understanding coats of arms

joust organized single combat, often fought on horseback with lances

mail armour formed of linked rings of metal

Mamluks Egyptian warriors

mêlée hand-to-hand fighting in the midst of battle

mercenary soldier prepared to serve any master for money

Moors Islamic peoples in Spain

muster the assembly of a troops at the start of a campaign, or for inspection

plate armour formed from metal sheets

quintain target for practising use of the lance

ransom payment for release of a prisoner

retinue the followers of an important person

reisen crusading expeditions in the Baltic

sally a counter-attack launched by those besieged in a castle or town

Saracen term used by crusaders for any non-Christian peoples

schiltrom tight infantry formation, employed by the Scots

sous tournois a form of French currency. There were 20 sous to a livre.

visor movable element of a helmet, which protects the face

Timeline

1302 Battle of Courtrai. Flemish infantry defeat the French army

1307 Battle of Loudoun Hill. Bruce's first significant victory over the English

1314 Battle of Bannockburn. Scottish victory against the English under Edward II

1315 Battle of Morgarten. Swiss success over Leopold of Austria

1317 Weardale campaign. Edward III's first campaign against the Scots, in the north of England

1328 Battle of Cassel. French victory over Flemish forces

1332 Battle of Dupplin Moor. English success against a larger Scottish army

1333 Battle of Halidon Hill. Victory for Edward III over the Scots

1339 French and English armies fail to engage at Buirenfosse

1340 Battle of Parabiago, near Milan. The Company of St George defeated by Milan

1340 Battle of Sluys. English naval victory in the Low Countries over the French fleet

1340 Failure of the English and their allies at the siege of Tournai

1344 Fall of Algeciras in Spain to crusading forces

1346 Battle of Crécy. English victory against the French

1346 Battle of Neville's Cross. King David II of Scots captured by the English

1352 Battle of Mauron. English victory against the French

1356 Battle of Poitiers. English victory which sees the capture of the French king John II

1360 Treaty of Brétigny between France and England

1367 Battle of Nájera in Spain between Peter of Castile, supported by the Black Prince, and forces backing Henry of Trastamara

1382 Battle of Roosebeke. French victory over the Flemings

1385 Battle of Aljubarrota. Victory for Portuguese, with English support, against a Franco-Castilian army

1387 Battle of Castagnaro. Paduan forces under John Hawkwood defeat Verona

1396 Battle of Nicopolis. Crusader forces defeated in the Balkans by the Ottoman Turks

1410 Battle of Tannenberg (Grunwald). Polish victory over the Teutonic Knights

1415 Battle of Agincourt. English victory over France

Further Reading

Anglo, S. *The Martial Arts of Renaissance Europe* (Yale University Press, New Haven and London, 2000)

Ayton, A and Preston, P. *The Battle of Crécy, 1346* (Boydell Press, Woodbridge, 2005)

Barber, R. and Barker, J. *Tournaments: Jousts, Chivalry and Pageants in the Middle Ages* (Boydell Press, Woodbridge, 1989)

R. Barber (ed.) *The Life and Campaigns of the Black Prince* (Boydell Press, Woodbridge, 1979)

Barker, J. *The Tournament in England 1100–1400* (Boydell Press, Woodbridge, 1986)

Bennett, M. (ed.) *The Medieval World at War* (Thames & Hudson, London and New York, 2009)

Boulton, D'A. J. D. *The Knights of the Crown: The Monarchical Orders of Knighthood in Later Medieval Europe 1325–1520* (Boydell Press, Woodbridge, 1987)

Caferro, W. *John Hawkwood: An English Mercenary in Fourteenth Century Italy* (The Johns Hopkins University Press, Baltimore, 2006)

Caferro, W. *Mercenary Companies and the Decline of Siena* (The Johns Hopkins University Press, Baltimore, 1998)

Christiansen, E. *The Northern Crusades: The Baltic and the Catholic Frontier 1100–1525* (The Macmillan Press, London, 1980)

Contamine, P. *Guerre, état et société à la fin du moyen age* (Mouton & Co., Paris, 1972)

Cooper, S. *Sir John Hawkwood: Chivalry and the Art of War* (Pen and Sword Books, Barnsley, 2008)

Curry, A. *Agincourt: A New History* (Tempus Publishing, Stroud, 2006)

Fowler, K. *The King's Lieutenant* (Elek books, London, 1969)

Fowler, K. *Medieval Mercenaries I: The Great Companies* (Blackwell, Oxford, 2002)

Given-Wilson, C., Kettle, A. and Scales, L. (eds), *War, Government and Aristocracy in the British Isles c. 1150–1500* (Boydell Press, Woodbridge, 2008)

Green, D. *The Battle of Poitiers 1356* (Tempus Publishing, Stroud, 2002)

Mathew, H. G. C. and Harrison, B. (eds) *Oxford Dictionary of National Biography* (Oxford University Press, Oxford, 2004)

Houseley, N. *The Later Crusades: From Lyons to Alcazar, 1274–1580* (Oxford University Press, Oxford, 1992)

Keen, M. H. *Nobles, Knights and Men-at-Arms in the Middle Ages* (Hambledon Continuum, London, 1996)

Keen, M. H. *Chivalry* (Yale University Press, New Haven and London, 1984)

Keen, M. H. *The Laws of War in the Late Middle Ages* (Routledge and Kegan Paul, London, 1965)

Kaeuper, R. W. *Chivalry and Violence in Medieval Europe* (Oxford University Press, Oxford, 1999)

Kaeuper, R. W. and Kennedy, E. (eds) *The Book of Chivalry of Geoffroi de Charny* (University of Pennsylvania Press, Philadelphia, 1996)

Lalande, D. *Jean II le Meingre, dit Boucicaut (1366–1421): Étude d'une biographie héroïque* (Librarie Droz, Geneva, 1988)

Mallet, M. *Mercenaries and their Masters: Warfare in Renaissance Italy* (The Bodley Head, London, 1974)

Muhlberger, S. *Deeds of Arms* (Chivalry Bookshelf, Highland Village, Texas, 2005)

Muhlberger, S. *Jousts and Tournaments: Charny and the Rules for Chivalric Sport in Fourteenth Century France* (Chivalry Bookshelf, Union City, California, 2002)

Prestwich, M. C. *Armies and Warfare in the Middle Ages: The English Experience* (Yale University Press, New Haven and London, 1996)

Rawcliffe, C. *Medicine and Society in Later Medieval England* (Alan Sutton, Stroud, 1995)

Rogers, C. J. *Soldiers Lives Through History: The Middle Ages* (Greenwood Press, Westport, Connecticut, 2007)

Rogers, C. J. *War, Cruel and Sharp* (Boydell Press, Woodbridge, 2000)

Selzer, S. *Deutsche Söldner im Italien des Trecento* (Niemeyer, Tübingen, 2001)

Sumption, J. *The Hundred Years War I: Trial by Battle* (Faber and Faber, London, 1990)

Sumption, J. *The Hundred Years War II: Trial by Fire* (Faber and Faber, London, 1999)

Vernier, R. *The Flower of Chivalry: Bertrand du Guesclin and the Hundred Years War* (Boydell Press, Woodbridge, 2003)

Wright, N. *Knights and Peasants: The Hundred Years War in the French Countryside* (Boydell Press, Woodbridge, 1998)

Websites

De Re Militari, at www.deremilitari.org/

Internet Medieval Sourcebook, at www.fordham.edu/halsall/sbook.html

Many works, such as editions of Froissart's chronicles, can be found at gallica.bnf.fr/

A wide-ranging site, with some useful links, is About.Com:Medieval History, at historymedren.about.com/

Film

Brian Helgeland, director and producer, *A Knight's Tale* (2001)

Sources of Quotations

N.B. All quotations from Chaucer are based on the text and translation at classiclit.about.com/od/chaucer geoffrey/Chaucer_Geoffrey.htm

Chapter 1

6 *The Book of Chivalry of Geoffroi de Charny*, ed. R. W. Kaeuper and E. Kennedy, 105

Chapter 2

13 H. Döbringer, *Fechtbuch*, trans. D. Lindholm, www.thearma.org/ Manuals/dobringer.html

14 Christine de Pizan, www.gutenberg.org/files/18061/

15 *The Book of Chivalry of Geoffroi de Charny*, ed. R. W. Kaeuper and E. Kennedy, 101

16 H. Döbringer, *Fechtbuch*

17 S. Anglo, *The Martial Arts of Renaissance Europe*, 8

17 G. Diaz de Gamez, *The Unconquered Knight*, trans. J. Evans (In Parentheses Publications, Cambridge, Ontario, 2000), 17

18 *The Book of Chivalry of Geoffroi de Charny*, ed. R. W. Kaeuper and E. Kennedy, 115

19 J. Barbour, *The Bruce*, ed. A. A. M. Duncan (Canongate Press, Edinburgh, 1997), 132

22 *Chroniques de Jean Froissart*, ed. S. Luce (Soc. de l'histoire de France, Paris, 1869) i, part ii, 2

Chapter 3

23 *Sir John Froissart's Chronicles of England, France, Spain*, ed. T. Johnes (William Smith, London, 1839), ii. 119

25 M. Mallet, *Mercenaries and their Masters: Warfare in Renaissance Italy*, 211

26 *Foedera, conventiones, litterae, et cujuscunque generis acta publica…*, ed. A. Clarke, F. Holbrooke and others (Record Commission, London, 1816–69) vii, 630

27 *The Book of Chivalry of Geoffroi de Charny*, ed. R. W. Kaeuper and E. Kennedy, 177

29 *Menestrellorum multitudo*, ed. C. Bullock-Davies, (University of Wales Press, Cardiff, 1978), xxiv

30 *The Life and Campaigns of the Black Prince*, ed. R. Barber, 118

31 Froissart *Chronicles*, ed. G. Brereton (Penguin, Harmondsworth, 1968), 72

32 *Testamenta Vetusta*, ed. N. H. Nicholas (Nichols & Son, London, 1826), 126

33 *The Life and Campaigns of the Black Prince*, ed. R. Barber, 86

Chapter 4

36 *Filippo Villani's Chronicle*, cited in G. R. Parks, *The English Traveler to Italy* (Stanford, 1954), www.deremilitari.org /resources/ sources/villani3.htm

45 *The Tree of Battles of Honoré Bouvet*, ed. G. W. Coopland, (Liverpool University Press, Liverpool, 1949) 121

46 *Middle English Verse Romances*, ed. D. B. Sands (University of Exeter Press, Exeter, 1986), 209

49 *The Book of Chivalry of Geffroi de Charny*, ed. R. W. Kaeuper and E. Kennedy, 171

50 *Sir John Froissart's Chronicles*, ed.
T. Johnes, i. 497

Chapter 5

54 Matteo Villani's *Chronicle*, cited in D'A.
J. D. Boulton, *The Knights of the Crown*,
217

55 *Chronicles of the Reigns of Edward I and
II*, ed. W. Stubbs (Rolls Series, London,
1882–3), i. 186, 192

57 (Knights of the Band) *Cronica del Rey
Don Alfonso el Onceno*, cited in
D'A. J. D. Boulton, *The Knights of the
Crown*, 53

57 (Order of the Round Table) *Chronique
de Jean le Bel*, ed. J. Viard and E. Déprez
(Renouard, Paris, 1905), ii. 26–7

60 D'A. J. D. Boulton, *The Knights of the
Crown*, 218, 297

62 Christine de Pizan,
www.gutenberg.org/files/18061/

Chapter 6

63 'Private Indentures for Life Service in
Peace and War 1278–1478', ed. M. Jones
and S. Walker, *Camden Miscellany
XXXII* (Royal Historical Society,
London, 1994), 70

73 *Song of Caerlaverock*,
www.deremilitari.org

75 'Private Indentures for Life Service', ed.
M. Jones and S. Walker, 61–2

76 *Calendar of Patent Rolls, 1346* (Public
Record Office, London), 126

78 J. Andoni Fernández de Larrea Rojas,
*Guerra y Sociedad en Navarra durante la
Edad Media* (Universidad del Pais Vasco,
Bilbao, 1992), 146

Chapter 7

79 *Vita Edwardi Secundi*, ed. W. Childs
(Oxford University Press, Oxford, 2005),
7

83, 85 Ulrich Von Liechtenstein, *Service of
Ladies*; trans. J. W. Thomas, (Boydell
Press, Woodbridge, 2004), 59, 64

88, 89 *The Chronicles of Enguerrand de
Monstrelet*, trans. T. Johnes (William
Smith, London, 1840), i. 5

Chapter 8

93 'The Vows of the Heron', in *Laurence
Minot Poems*, ed. T. B. James and
J. Simons (Exeter Medieval English
Texts and Studies, Exeter, 1989), 79

96, 97 *The Song of Caerlaverock*, at
www.deremilitari.org

98 (Throwing himself on a bed) Pere III
of Catalonia/Peter IV of Aragon,
Chronicle, trans. M. Hillgarth (Pontifical
Institute of Medieval Studies, Toronto,
1980), ii. 561

98 (Rotten food) *The Unconquered
Knight*, G. Diaz de Gamez, 6

98 (Animals to eat) Pere III of
Catalonia/Peter IV of Aragon, *Chronicle*,
263

100 (Black Prince's raid) *Life and
Campaigns of the Black Prince*, ed.
R. Barber, 50

100 (Pedro IV of Aragon) Pere III of
Catalonia/Peter IV of Aragon, *Chronicle*,
i. 204

101 *The Chronicle of Jean de Venette*, ed.
R. Newhall, trans. J. Birdsall (Columbia
University Press, New York. 1953), 95

102 *The Tree of Battles*, ed. G. W.
Coopland, 153

Chapter 9

112 (Boucicaut's expedition) *Le Livre des
Fais du Bon Messire Jehan le Maingre dit
Boucicaut, Mareschal de France et
Gouverneur de Jenes*, ed. D. Lalande
(Librairie Droz, Geneva, 1985), 77

113 N. Houseley, *The Later Crusades*, 327

Chapter 10

117 W. Caferro, *John Hawkwood: An English Mercenary in Fourteenth Century Italy*, 178

117 *The Book of Chivalry of Geoffroi de Charny*, ed. R. W. Kaeuper and E. Kennedy, 93

124 W. Caferro, *Mercenary Companies and the Decline of Siena*, 36

Chapter 11

126 'The Vows of the Heron', in *Laurence Minot Poems*, ed. T. B. James and J. Simons, 79

128 *Medieval English Verse*, trans. B. Stone (Penguin, Harmondsworth, 1964), 202

131 *Froissart Chronicles*, ed. G. Brereton, 162

132 B. Muhlberger, *Jousts and Tournaments*, 25

134 (Prowess in the bedroom) 'Knights of Venus', W. M. Ormrod, *Medium Aevum* 73 (2004), 290

134 (William Gold's heartbreak) *Chronicon Henrici Knighton*, ii, ed. J. R. Lumby (Rolls Series, London, 1895), 58

135 *Calendar of State Papers and Manuscripts relating to English Affairs Existing in the Archives of Venice and Other Libraries of Northern Italy*, ed. H. F. Brown and A. B. Hind, i (London, 1864), 24

Chapter 12

136 *Gesta Henrici Quinti*, ed. and trans. F. Taylor and J. S. Roskell (Oxford University Press, Oxford, 1975), 39

137 *The Song of Caerlaverock*, www.deremilitari.org

140 *Liber Quotidianus Contrarotulatoris Garderobae*, ed. J. Topham and others (Society of Antiquaries of London, London, 1987), 70

146 *Sir John Froissart's Chronicles*, ed. T. Johnes, i. 454

Chapter 13

148 *The Life and Campaigns of the Black Prince*, ed. Richard Barber, 126

152 *The Life and Campaigns of the Black Prince*, ed. Richard Barber, 74–5

152 W. Caferro, *John Hawkwood*, 11

162, 163 *The Bruce*, ed. A. A. M. Duncan, 19, 302, 476

168 (Aljubarrota) *Sir John Froissart's Chronicles*, ed. T. Johnes, ii. 121, i. 121

168 *The Bruce*, ed. A. A. M. Duncan, 486–8

169 *Gesta Henrici Quinti*, ed. F. Taylor and J. S. Roskell, 91

170 (Jan Dlugosz) www.deremilitari.org

171 (Audley's heroism) *Sir John Froissart's Chronicles*, ed. T. Johnes, i. 221

171 (Deyncourt) *The Bruce*, ed. A. A. M. Duncan, 434.

171 (Giles of Argentein) *The Bruce*, ed. A. A. M. Duncan, 494

171 (Felton) *The Lives and Campaigns of the Black Prince*, ed. Richard Barber, 120

Chapter 14

174 *Froissart Chronicles*, ed G. Brereton, 161

181 S. Cooper, *Sir John Hawkwood: Chivalry and the Art of War*, 97

183 'Private Indentures for Life Service in Peace and War 1278–1478', ed. M. Jones and S. Walker, 107

Chapter 15

186 *The Tree of Battles*, ed. G. W. Coopland, 156

188, 189 *Testamenta Vetusta*, ed. N. H. Nicolas, 134

190 P. Binski, *Medieval Death: Ritual and Representation* (British Museum Press, London, 1996), 67

Sovrces of Illvstrations

From *Address to Robert of Anjou, King of Naples, from the town of Prato in Tuscany,*
  c. 1335-40. British Library, London 65a
Biblioteca Nazionale Marciana, Venice. Photo Alfredo Dagli Orti/Art Archive,
  London 154a
Bibliothèque Nationale, Paris 66, 71, 165
Bibliothèque Nationale, Paris. Photo akg-images, London 61
From Giovanni Boccaccio, *On Famous Men and Women,* 15th century. Bibliothèque
  de l'Arsenal, Paris. Photo Art Archive, London 153
Bodleian Library, Oxford 129
From *Book of the Order at Burgos,* 14th century. Archivo Municipal, Burgos, Spain 56
Photo Bridgeman Art Library, London/Neil Holmes 58
British Library, London 67a, 74, 83l, 101, 156-157, 169
British Museum, London 67b, 130, 160
From Geoffrey Chaucer, *The Canterbury Tales* from the Ellesmere Mss., 1400-10.
  Huntington Library, San Marino, California 21
From Geoffrey Chaucer, *The Canterbury Tales,* Westminster, ?1485. British Library,
  London 109
From *Les Chroniques de France,* 14th century. British Library, London 8
From *Les Chroniques de France* or *Les Chroniques de Saint Denis,* 14th century. British
  Library, London 9, photo Bridgeman Art Library, London 55
From *Codex Manesse,* Zurich, *c.* 1310-40. University Library, Heidelberg 72b, 133,
  photo akg-images, London 160b
College of Arms, London 32
Photo Corbis, London/Dallas and John Heaton/Free Agents Limited 37
From Godefroy de Bouillon, *Crusades.* Bibliothèque Nationale, Paris. Photo Getty
  Images, London 7
From Chanson de Geste, early 14th century. British Library, London 28
From Christine de Pizan, *Livre des Faits d'Armes et de Chevalerie,* 15th century.
  Bibliothèque Nationale, Paris 2, 52
From Christine de Pizan, *Collected Works,* 1420. British Library, London. Photo akg-
  images, London 14
From Decretals of Gregory IX, 14th century. British Library, London 18-19
From Jean de Wavrin, *Chronique d'Angleterre,* Bruges, late 15th century. British
  Library, London 155a
From Jean de Froissart, *Chroniques,* 15th century. Bibliothèque Nationale, Paris 149,
  150, 154b, 158b
From Jean de Froissart, *Chroniques,* 15th century. British Library, London 70, 70-71, 155b

From a translation of Froissart by T. Johnes, 1839 88b, 110, 175, 192

Hawking, from *Traites de Fauconnerie et de Venerie*, 1459. Musée Condé, Chantilly 69

From *Histoire du petit Jehan de Saintre*, 15th century. British Museum, London 80, 85

From Sir Thomas Holmes's Book, *c.* 1443. British Library, London 82

From Sir Thomas Holmes's Book, *c.* 1445. British Library, London. Photo Bridgeman Art Library, London 83r

From a hunting book by Gaston Phebus, Burgundy, 1407. Bibliothèque Nationale, Paris 68

Nick Jakins © Thames & Hudson Ltd., London 27, 33, 47, 48, 49, 50, 142, 182, 185l

From the *Journey of Marco Polo*, *c.* 1410–20. Bodleian Library, Oxford 138

From the Luttrell Psalter, 14th century. British Library, London 65b, photo akg-images, London 127, photo Bridgeman Art Library, London 99

Metropolitan Museum of Art, New York 38

Musée du Louvre, Paris. Photo Art Archive, London 187

Musée Goya, Castres, France 141

Museum of London 4–5

Palazzo Pubblico, Siena 95a, 121

From A. Parmentier, *Album Historique,* Paris 1895 1, 42, 45, 53, 77, 81, 86, 87, 88a, 90, 91, 95b, 97, 114, 123, 144, 163, 170, 177, 185r, 189

From Ralph Payne-Gallwey, *The Crossbow*, 1903 51

Pierpont Morgan Library, New York 43

Photo Michael Prestwich 137

From *The Romance of Alexander, c.* 1338-44. Bodleian Library, Oxford 167

From Saint Alban's *Chronicle*, 15th century. Lambeth Palace Library, London 158–59

San Francesco, Bagnacavallo 17

SMPK, Geheimes Staatsarchiv, Berlin. Photo akg-images, London 176

From a treatise of surgery by Roger of Salerno, *c.* 1300. British Library, London 105

Tower of London 40

University Library, Heidelberg. Photo akg-images, London 72a

Victoria & Albert Museum, London 188l

Warwick Castle, Warwick 39

Westley Waterless, Cambridgeshire/ Monumental Brass Society 188r

Ïпdex

Page numbers in *italics*
indicate illustrations

Acre 54, 56, 109
Alexandria 111, 185
Alfonso XI, king of Castile,
 89, 112
al-Mahdiya 110–1, *155*
appatis 181
archers 46, 52, *52*, 64, 123,
 151–2, 165–8, *167, 169*
Arderne, John of 105
Argentein, Giles of 91, 109,
 171
armour 36–41, *37–40, 42,
 43–4*, 46, 53, 82
Arthur, king of Britain 7,
 15, 34, *66*
astrology 94
Audley, James 24, 170, 172
Avignon 38, 44, 181

bannerets 34–5
banners *74, 81, 87*, 96, 103
Barbiano, Alberigo da 121
barbuta 64, 123
Basset, Ralph, lord of
 Drayton 22, 32, 187
baths 28, 83, *72*, 105, 112, 186
battle Agincourt 9, 11, 26,
 150, 152, *158*–9, 167, 169,
 177, 179, 185; Aljubarrota
 23, 30, 116, 165, 168–9,
 169; Auray 27, 53, 161,
 162, 168, 175, 180, 184;
 Bannockburn 9, 34, 50,
 146, 151, 161, 164, 170, 171,
 173; Brignais 120, 184;
 Buirenfosse 31, 148;
 Cassel 164; Castagnaro
 123, 151, 168, 172;

Courtrai *8, 9*, 73, 164,
 175; Crécy *8, 9*, 10, 33, 57,
 78, 93, 150–1, *150*, 161,
 164, 166, 168, 170, 172,
 173; Dupplin Moor 166,
 169; Fight of the Thirty
 161; Halidon Hill 107,
 166; Launac 177; Laupen
 164; Les Espagnols sur
 Mer 20; Loudoun Hill
 151; Mauron 59, 172;
 Morgarten 10, 164;
 Morlaix 10; Nájera 27,
 33, 35, 162, 164, 171, 173,
 179–80; Neville's Cross
 9, *165*, 168, 178;
 Nicopolis 11, 111, 148–9,
 151, 161, 165, 172, 179–80;
 Nogent-sur-Seine 40;
 Parabiago 93, 119;
 Poitiers 9, 11, 31, 33, 59,
 93, 123, *149*, 151–2, *158*,
 161, 164, 167–8, 170, 177,
 184; Roosebeke 9, 11, 30,
 34, 50, 164, 172; Sempach
 10, 165, 176; Shrewsbury
 105; Tannenberg 56, 113,
 170, 176
Bāyazīd, Ottoman Sultan
 (1389–1402), 111, 115, 166
Beauchamp, Thomas, earl
 of Warwick 63
Beaumanoir, Jean de 161,
 175
Bel, Jean le *37*, 57
Berwick 29, 144
Black Prince *see* Edward
Blois, Charles of 178
Bohun, Henry de 50
Bolingbroke, Henry *see*
 Henry IV

Bongard, Haneken 78,
 119–20, 134, 181, 185
Boniface VIII, Pope
 (1294–1303) 190
Book of Chivalry see
 Charny
Book of Holy Medicine 19
booty 79, 111, 114, 174,
 181–2, *182*, 185
Bordeaux 52, 186
Boucicaut (Jean II le
 Maingre) battles 50,
 150, 148, 165, 172; career
 11, 15–16, 30, 35, 62, 111,
 180–1, 184, 190–1;
 character 26, 73, 99, 103,
 128, 135, 187; childhood
 13, 19–21; crusades 112,
 114, 165; jousts 86, 91;
 sieges 138, 140–1
Bourbon, Louis duke of
 59, *110*, 191
Bouvet, Honoré 45, 76,
 102, 186
brotherhood-in-arms 74
Bruce, Robert, king of
 Scots (1306–29) 19,
 50, 112, 151, 162, 168,
 173, 190

Caen 128, 181
Calais 10, 86–7, 97
Calveley, Constança 132
Calveley, Hugh 24, 32, 53,
 74, 104, 132, 161–2, 183–4
camp 94–6, *95*
cannibalism 102
Captal de Buch *see* Grailly
Cesena 125, 129
Chandos Herald 30, 33,
 148, 191

Chandos, John 31, 35, 175, 180, *192*
Charles V, king of France (1364–80) 64, *70*, 76, 180
Charles VI, king of France (1380–1422) *71*, 106
Charny, Geoffroi de 33, 49, 92, 116; *Book of Chivalry* 6, 10–12, 14–15, 18, 20, 174, 180; career 10–11, 111; on battle 79, 148, 161; on knighting 27–9; on mercenaries 117; on profits of war 174; on women 126, 128, 134–5
Chaucer, Geoffrey 21, 82, 95, 108
chevauchée 98, 100
chivalry 23, 31, 33–6, 124–5, 171
Clement V, Pope (1305–14) 190
Clement VII, Anti-Pope (1378–94) 116
Clifford, Robert 73
clothing 29, 41, 43, 58, 61, 76, 92, 134, 191
coats of arms 31–2, 46
Colville, Robert 107
condotta 76
condottieri 11, 118–25
constable, office of 24, 27, 35, 92, 103, 122, 185
Coupland, John of 178
cross-dressing 83, 132, 139, 190
crusade 10, 108–16, *114*

d'Auberchicourt, Eustace 40, 131, 133, 174, 176, 180
Dammartin, count of 177, 180
Datini, Francesco 38, 44
David II, king of Scots

(1329–71) 9, 178
De Fistula in Ano 105
Derby, earl of 112, 131
Devil, the 28
discipline 102–4
Douglas Castle 130
Douglas, James 112, 190
Douglas, William 167
Dubois, Pierre 110

Edinburgh Castle 139
Edward I, king of England (1272–1307) 13, 89, 96–7, 129, 143
Edward II, king of England (1307–27) 18
Edward III, king of England (1327–77) 30, 53, 67, 76–7, 90; alleged rape of countess of Salisbury 130; campaigns 20, 149, 170, 175; orders of chivalry 57, 59; pardons 26, 76; tournaments, 89–90
Edward the Black Prince 33, 35, 164, 191; battles 152, 171, 179; campaigns 25, 98; career 20, 30, 33; retinue 64; sieges 125, 146
Eu, count of 177
exchange rates 178

Feast of the Heron 131
Fechtbuch 13, 16
fencing 16–17
Florence 10–11, 76, 91, 118, 189
Fogliano, Guidoriccio da 121, *121*
Foix, Gaston, count of 67, 100, 112, 129
food and drink 94, 98, 99–100, 125, 144–5, 153
Froissart, Jean 22, 35, 50,

135, 146, 170, 174, 177, 183–4, 190
Garter, order of the 57, 58, *58*, 60, 62, 191
Gaunt, John of, duke of Lancaster 20, 77, 148
Gdansk 112, 115
Genoa 11, 184, 191
Gloucester, earl of 34, 161, 171
gods 27, 58, 108, 115, 146, 148, 172
Gold, William 104, 134
Grailly, Jean de (the Captal de Buch) 129, 164, 186
Granada 24, 108, 112
Gray, Thomas, the elder 46, 145
Gray, Thomas, the younger 19
Grosmont, Henry of, duke of Lancaster 19, 128
guastatori 122, 181
Guesclin, Bertrand du 27, 73, *155*, 162, 188, 191; captured 179–80; career 24, 26–7, 35; character 50; retinue 64, 73; sieges 104, 139
gunpowder 144

Hawkwood, Donnina 133
Hawkwood, John 94, 101, 116, *118*, 120, 134; battles 123, 168; career 11, 34; character 104, 152; children 135; relations with Italian cities 76, 78, 118, 177, 181, 185, 189; sieges 122–3, 125, 129
heaven 186
hell 186
Henry IV, king of England (1399–1413) 114–16
Henry V, king of England

(1413–22) 20, 89, 100,
103, 140, 145, 149, 152, 177
heraldry 15, 31–2, *32*
Hereford, earl of 75, 161
horses 17, 18, 22, 45–7, *45,
47*, 84, 98, 144–5, 131
hunting 18, *18*, 68–9, 113

Isabeau of Bavaria, queen
of France 90

Janet, mistress of William
Gold 134–5
Jerusalem 109
João, king of Portugal
(1385–1433) 23, 30
John II, king of France
(1350–64) 59
John of Luxembourg, king
of Bohemia (1310–46) 90
jousts 72, 80, *80*, 82–9, *82,
85*

Knollys, Constance 133
Knollys, Robert 24, 74,
103–4, 132–3, 182–3, 187
Knot, company of the
60–1, *61*
Königsberg 114–15

Lancaster, duke of *see*
Gaunt; Grosmont
Landau, Conrad of
119–20, 124
Latimer, William (d. 1327)
135
Latimer, William (d. 1381)
146
laws of war 8, 125
Liechtenstein, Ulrich von
83, 84, 85, *160*, 190
Limoges 33, 125, 146, 147
Limousin 135
Lithuania 10, 56, 108, 114,
116

Llull, Ramon 20, 26
Louis, duke of Bourbon
111, 139
love 21, 79, 83, 107, 126–8,
130–1, 133–4, 174
Lovel, William 76
Ludwig IV, Emperor
(1328–47) 119
Luttrell, Geoffrey 65
Luxembourg, John of, king
of Bohemia (1310–4) 173

Mamluks 109, 112
Marienburg 112, 114
marriage 132–3, 135
marshal, office of 35
Mauléon, Bascot de 139,
183, 184
Mauny, Walter 135, 179,
187, 189
Meaux 129, 184
mêlée 79, 81, 163–4, 16–72
mercenary companies 11,
119–22, 181
Mézières, Philippe de 109
Milan 10, 11, 38, 118, 191
Mondeville, Henri de 104,
106
Montague, William, earl of
Salisbury 92
Montferrand 140
Montpellier 104
Mugnano di Creta 101
Murad I, Ottoman Sultan
(1359–89) 109, 111
murder 134
muster 94

Naples 10, 145
Narbonne 98
Navarre 75
Niño, Pero 17, 24, 106
Norham Castle 130
Norwich, bishop of 116,
145, 162

nun, attractive 104
orders of chivalry 10–11,
54–62, 89, 128, 172, 191
see also Garter, Knot
Oriflamme 11
Orthez 183
Ottoman Turks 109, 111

Padua 94, 123, 134
pay 74–8, 94, 117, 119, 124
peasants 25, 33, 79, 101–2,
101, 128–9, 181, 184, 191
Peasants' Revolt 24, 104
Pedro IV, king of Aragon
(1336–87) 46, 78, 98,
100, 164, 190
Perrers, Alice 90
Peter I, king of Cyprus
(1358–69) 111
Philip IV, king of France
(1285–1314) 55, 89
Philip VI, king of France
(1328–50) 92, 131, 149,
175
Pizan, Christine de 12, 14,
14, 19, 62
plague 106
Poinz, Hugh 31
polygamy 113
Ponthieu 73
Pont-Saint-Esprit 120
Prato 38
Prendergast, John 89
Prussia 113, 114

Quenillart, Henry 176
quintain 16

ransoms 10, 12, 81, 101, 103,
171, 173–5, *175*, 177–80,
185, 191
Raoul, count of Eu 92
Reims 98
Rennes 27
resurrection 190

retines 64, 73
Rhineland 117
Rhodes 110, 115
Ribblesdale, fair maid of 128
Richard II, king of England (1377–99) 13, 26, 103, 189
Round Table 90
Roxburgh 129
Roye, Renaud de 86, 87
Roye, Tristan de 107

St James of Santiago, order of 56, *56*
saddles 47, 48
Salisbury, countess of 130
Salisbury, earl of 112, 131, 180
Salonica 110
Sardinia 146, 164
Scalacronica 19
Scrope *v*. Grosvenor 31
siege Algeciras 108, 112; Berwick 144; Bothwell 143; Brest 145; Caerlaverock 136–7, 140–1; Calais 147; Harfleur 140, 145, 149; Iglesias 144, 146; Melun 104; Montignac 141; Reims 147; St Sauveur 146; Stirling Castle 146; Tournai 147; Vertueil 139
siege engines belfry 143, *143*; *couillard* 141–2, *141*; guns 141, 144; sow 143, *143*; springald 142, 145; trebuchet 140, 141–2, *142*, 145
siege techniques blockade 144–5; mining 139–40; scaling ladders 138, *138*;

surprise attack 139
Siena 78, 95, 117, 118, 181, 185
Sigismund, king of Hungary (1387–1437) 111, 161
sins, seven deadly 90
Sir Launfal 46
Song of Caerlaverock 73, 96, 97, 137
squires 21, *21*, 22, 26
St Inglevert 70, 86–7
Sterz, Albert 120, 181, 185
surgery 104–6, *105*
Swabia 117
swimming 19

Tancarville, Raoul count of 177, 185
Templars 54–5, *55*, 60
tents 95–6, *95*
Teutonic Knights 10, 56, 112–14, *176*
Thweng, Lucy 135
Timur 109, 115
tombs 188–9, *188–9*
Topaz, Sir 94–5
tournament 41, 79, 81–2, 87, 89–9, 132
Tree of Battles 102, 186
trumpets 82, 96

Urban VI, Pope (1378–89) 116
Urslingen, Werner of 118, 119, 121

Vegetius 19, 94
Venette, Jean de 101
Venice 10, 115
Verona 123
Vicomte, Renaud le 178
Vienna 115

Villani, Filippo 36
Villani, Matteo 54
Visconti, Ambrogio 121
vows 88, 130–1, *130*, 170, 172–3, 191
Vows of the Heron 93, 126
Vytautas, ruler of Lithuania 113

Warenne, John de, earl of Surrey 20, 135
weapons arrows 53; axe 50, *50*, 88, 172; crossbow 18, 51, *51*, 141; dagger 88; falchion 50; guns 172; halberd 53, *53*; lance 16, 48, *48*, 64, 49, 86, 88, 123; longbow 18, 51–2, *52*, 167; mace 50; pole weapons 52–3; swords 16, 49–50, *49*, *77*, 88, *170*
Weardale campaign 20, 96
Westminster Abbey 30, 179
Windsor Castle 57
women anatomy 127; aristocratic 62, 128; methods of persuasion used by 130–1; mistresses 90, 132, 134–5; of easy virtue 134, 185; perfect 127, *127*; put in cages 129; saved from dreadful fate 128–9; services provided by 122; tournaments 90–1, 131–2

York, duke of 183